How to Grow
African Violets

By the Editors of Sunset Books and Sunset Magazine

LANE PUBLISHING CO. ● MENLO PARK, CALIFORNIA

Foreword

Because intensive cultivation of African violets really began in this century, most knowledge about them is of recent origin—and the multitude of excellent hybrids are also recent. That so much has been done in a relatively short time is a testimony to the attraction these flowers possess.

Work on this book was made easier by the selfless cooperation of various African violet growers who have long been captured by this attraction. We would like to give thanks to Buell's Greenhouses, Eastford, CT; Ruth Carey, Knoxville, TN; Fischer Greenhouses, Linwood, NJ; Grace Foote, Port Arthur, TX; Madeline Gonzales, San Jose, CA; Kartuz Greenhouses, Wilmington, MA; Lyndon Lyon, Dolgeville, NY; Edith V. Peterson, San Francisco, CA; Betty Stoehr, Greenwood, IN; Sunnyside Nurseries, Hayward, CA; Tinari Greenhouses, Huntingdon Valley, PA; and Alma Wright, Knoxville, TN.

Also of invaluable aid were the African Violet Society of America and its publication, *The African Violet Magazine;* and the American Gesneria Society and the Saintpaulia International and their bimonthly journal, *Gesneriad-Saintpaulia News.* We wish to extend special thanks to photographer Ells Marugg who—with one exception—took all of the color photographs, and to Philip Edinger and Joe Seals for their editorial contributions.

Supervising Editor: Kathryn L. Arthurs

Research and Text: Jack Kramer

Design: Steve Reinisch

Illustrations: Terrence Meagher

Cover: The variety of form and color in the African violet family is illustrated by these three plants. Two are modern African violet hybrids: 'Mighty Mini' (top right), though the name seems to imply so, is not a miniature; 'Midget Valentine' (bottom) is a true miniature. The hanging plant at the left is *Streptocarpus saxorum,* a popular "gesneriad" or colorful cousin to the African violet. Photographed by Ells Marugg.

Editor, Sunset Books: Elizabeth L. Hogan

Seventh printing November 1988

Contents

Special Features

The African Violet: A Star Is Born

Have you been searching for a house plant that will give you flowers throughout the year, that will not outgrow its bounds, and that will grow happily in the same temperature and humidity ranges that you, too, prefer? Then you ought to consider growing African violets in your home.

Not only do African violets satisfy the foregoing requirements, but they are also available in a great variety of colors, foliage types, and styles of flowers so that there is always something new to keep your interest and enthusiasm going. Furthermore, they can be used indoors in many ways (see pages 22-29), including—in addition to the traditional plant displays at windows—groupings under fluorescent lights in any part of any room.

Along with all these advantages, they are inexpensive—and so easy to propagate that in no time at all you can grow enough new plants to more than satisfy your own needs and those of your friends as well.

Their African Beginnings . . .

The resemblance of these flowers to true violets is partially responsible for the popular name "African violets" by which these plants are known; the "African" part of the name does, indeed, reflect the continent of their origin. Botanically these plants are called *Saintpaulia;* the most important species are described on pages 7-8. In the larger sense, African violets (Saintpaulias) belong to the family Gesneriaceae, which includes a number of other popular house plants (such as the florists' gloxinias) that you will meet in the chapter beginning on page 48.

In two separate locations in northeast Tanzania, African violets were discovered and collected by a German colonial official and planter—the Baron von Saint Paul—in 1892. Records are unclear as to whether he sent plants or seeds to his father in northern Germany, but in either case plants flowered there in 1893—for the first time outside their native Africa.

Upon seeing these plants in flower, the director of the Royal Botanic Garden at Herrenhausen realized that they were a new find in the plant world and named the plants *Saintpaulia* in honor of the father and son who discovered and grew them. The species then flowering he named *ionantha,* which means "with violetlike flowers." Within only a few years after its introduction to horticultural circles, the African violet was being grown and offered for sale by several European seed and plant firms.

During this period (still before 1900) a sharp-eyed grower noticed that some of the plants produced seed capsules that were long and slender, while others had rounded capsules. Not until well into this century was it realized that the Baron von Saint Paul had sent *two* species to his father. Those with rounded capsules are now recognized as *Saintpaulia ionantha,* while the long-fruited species was appropriately designated *S. confusa.*

. . . And How They Grew

Although African violet plants had been introduced to this country shortly after their discovery, they made no particular impact among greenhouse and house plant fanciers. Very likely this was because the early growers in America

Simple but elegant *end-table setting features well-grown African violet in glazed ceramic pot. When out of bloom, plant can be replaced with one that has been growing in brighter light.*

'Norseman' is one of the original ten hybrids from Armacost & Royston. The very blue flowers bloom profusely above velvety foliage.

knew so little of how to care for these exotics that the plants gave up in despair. However, in 1927 the Los Angeles nursery firm of Armacost & Royston, Inc. imported African violet seeds from an English seed house and from the one in Germany which 30 years earlier had noticed the seed capsule differences. Something in the neighborhood of 1,000 plants were grown from these seeds; selections from these seedlings launched the African violet popularity wave that to this day is still growing.

Originally there were 10 selections from the Armacost and Royston plants. Of the German seedlings, two were given names: 'Blue Boy' and 'Sailor Boy'. 'Admiral', 'Amethyst', 'Commodore', 'Mermaid', 'Neptune', 'Norseman', 'No. 32', and 'Viking' came from the English seed. All were in the violet-purple-blue color range.

Though newer selections show considerable variation from these originals, some of these first 10 hybrids still compare favorably with others in their color classes. Some African violet shows have special categories for exhibiting these first hybrids.

The African violet we know today is a product of intensive hybridization, but most of this involves only the two species that were once thought to be one—and that were in the background of the Armacost & Royston hybrids.

The first differences in flower and foliage forms arose as mutations from named varieties (see page 9). Subsequent crosses of these with other named varieties established the mutant characteristics (doubleness, for example) and afforded new combinations of foliage, color, and form. The Fringette series, which came from the Fischer Greenhouses years ago, were the first flowers to have frilled and ruffled petals. The Fantasy line has blossoms of one color streaked or splotched with another. The duPont strain has thick, hairy, quilted leaves and very large flowers (though fewer of them). The newer Rhapsodie series is noted for its abundant growth and bloom.

The variations continue to go on and on so that now there is an almost infinite variety of flower form and coloring and leaf texture. Some blossoms resemble buttercups, others are star-shaped. There are varieties with flowers of snowy white, all shades of pink, crimson red, wine, and purple red, and all conceivable variations and intensities in the original blue and purple colors.

Departing from the solid colors, you can find flowers that are delicately edged with red, blue, or white (or even green); others may be irregularly splashed with color; still others may have darker centers that fade out to the petal edges or may have upper petal lobes darker than the lower ones. And to compound the possibilities, all these color arrangements may appear (depending upon the particular variety) in flowers that are single, semidouble, or fully double.

In addition to concentrating on improving flower colors and color combinations, hybridizers have been busy developing different growth habits. While there always have been certain varieties that would, with good care, make plants considerably larger than others in a collection, the production of definitely miniature varieties establishes the greatest size difference. These plants, and the somewhat larger semiminiatures, are perfect scaled-down replicas of full-size African violets—available in just about the same variety of colors, and great space savers where growing room is limited. Fewer in number than the miniature varieties but just as distinct a departure in plant habit are the hybrids which will trail over the edges of pots instead of

Comparison *of African violet forms includes*
standard (**at top**), *over 8 inches across;*
semi-miniature (**at center**), *6 to 8 inches; and trailer*
(**at bottom**).

forming compact rosettes. Most of these hybrids
probably stem from the species *S. grotei* which is
a naturally trailing sort.

Introducing the Wild Ones

The African violet species—all native to hills and
mountains of East Africa—may at first seem
somewhat unexciting if you compare them to
some of the ruffled, fringed, double, and mul-
ticolored hybrids. But if you look at them
alongside hybrids to which they are more directly comparable (single blue or violet flowers)
you may be surprised by how good some of them
look for plants that have not been "improved" by
man. At the very least you will find them interesting, and part of this interest stems from the
knowledge that presumably just two species (*S.
ionantha* and *S. confusa*) are in the ancestry of
nearly all modern hybrids and are responsible for
the almost incredible divergence from wild

flower and foliage types. It's hard not to wonder
what new characteristics might lie hidden in the
other species, awaiting only some enterprising
hybridizers to bring them to light.

Here are brief descriptions of each of the most
important species now recognized.

S. confusa bears clusters of deep violet flowers above medium to light green leaves that are
smooth, flat, and slightly quilted. It shows off
best when allowed to develop multiple crowns;
otherwise it is a small plant that will tend to grow
at an angle toward the side of its pot.

S. difficilis is easily grown as a single-crowned
plant; the leaves are definitely veined, long-
pointed, often spooned, and carried at the ends
of long, upright-growing leaf stalks. Flowers are
medium to deep blue.

S. diplotricha forms small single-crowned
rosettes of deep green to purplish green thick
leaves, paler on their undersides. Flowers are a
very pale blue lilac that approaches white.

S. goetziana is reputed to be difficult to grow,
requiring cool temperature, high humidity, and
subdued light. This is another trailing species
which sends up numerous rosettes of small dark
leaves from a creeping stem, so that the general
effect is pincushionlike. Flowers are such a pale
lavender that they are nearly white.

S. grandifolia grows as a rather large single-
crowned plant—the long leaf stalks angle upward and carry thin-textured, oval, medium
green leaves. The large clusters of violet flowers
are very showy.

S. grotei is the best known of the trailing
species, the stems of which may reach lengths of
3 feet on well grown plants. Flat, medium green
leaves are borne on the ends of distinctive brown
leaf stalks. Flowers are blue violet with darker
centers. Give plants shade and much moisture
but perfect drainage.

S. intermedia grows either as a single or
multiple-crowned plant with an upright habit.
The nearly round olive green leaves have a tendency to spoon. It produces its blue flowers with
no special care.

S. ionantha, like *S. confusa*, appears to be in
the background of modern hybrids. It bears blue
violet flowers, and the leaves are dark green and
quilted, with serrated edges. Growth is single-
crowned and upright.

Famous ancestor *of nearly all named hybrids is* Saintpaulia ionantha, *producing variable blue blossoms.*

S. magungensis is another trailing species. It has small, rounded to heart-shaped leaves which tend to cup under slightly and are much paler on their undersides. Flowers are a medium blue violet shading to darker centers. One form of this species, *S. m. amaniensis*, is often listed as a separate species.

S. nitida is a small species with shiny dark leaves and dark blue violet flowers. The leafstalks are slender, flexible, and brown to purplish green.

S. orbicularis grows best as a multiple-crowned plant. The rounded shiny dark green leaves with their purplish brown leaf stalks contrast nicely with the small light lilac, dark-centered blooms. In its native habitat it is subjected to more extremes of heat and coolness than other species.

S. pendula is still another trailing species but with nearly round gray green foliage—flat and with serrated edges. Its medium lavender blue flowers appear singly or in clusters of two.

S. pusilla is the smallest of the species and a true miniature. Leaves have purple undersides, and its tiny flowers are bicolored—upper lobes are blue but lower lobes are white.

S. rupicola has oval, scalloped leaves forming a rosette. Up to 6 purple blooms appear on each stem.

S. shumensis is another miniature which forms many crowns of small, almost round olive green leaves. Its small flowers are nearly white with contrasting violet centers. Because its native habitat is quite dry, this species is sensitive to overwatering.

S. teitensis grows in a rosette with long leaf stems and almost round, scalloped leaves. Short flower spikes produce 1-inch violet flowers.

S. tongwensis is another like *S. confusa* which can be grown as a single-crowned plant but with a definite tendency to lean over and grow toward the pot's edge. The large, somewhat heart-shaped leaves have a distinctive lighter central streak; light blue flowers are profusely produced, particularly at high temperatures.

S. velutina has velvety, scalloped, heart-shaped leaves—dark green above and red purple underneath. Above these are carried pale blue, dark-eyed flowers. Plants form very attractive, single-crowned and fairly flat rosettes. This species also is sensitive to overwatering.

African Violet Terms to Remember

The considerable variation you find in African violet flowers and foliage—both in color and shapes—has brought forth a list of descriptive terms particular to these plants. Some of these terms are self-explanatory; those that aren't were coined from the name of the variety that first exhibited the characteristic.

The photograph below shows many but not all of the possible foliage and flower variations. The first descriptions refer to the photograph (background grid is 1-inch squares).

1. Plain leaf, sometimes called "boy" foliage after the variety 'Blue Boy'.
2. "Girl" leaf, named for the hybrid 'Blue Girl' which was a mutation from 'Blue Boy'; distinguishing feature is the white spot at the leaf base.
3. Oak leaf, with slightly indented margins.
4. Quilted leaf, with distinctly raised areas between leaf veins.
5. Fluted leaf.
6. Serrated leaf edge.
7. Variegated leaf—green and cream white.
8. Black green leaf.
9. A heavily rippled leaf, almost bordering on fringe.
10. Holly-type foliage.

A. Plain, single flower typical of the species and most of the early hybrids.
B. Semi-double flower has a few extra petaloids but stamens are clearly visible.
C. Single "star" flower, easy to recognize because of the five equally spaced and sized petals.
D. Double flower has additional full-size petals.
E. Single fringed flower. Petal edges are comparable to the leaf edge of number 9.
F. Multicolor double flower—petals and edges are two different colors.
G. Fringed double flower.
H. Crested double flower, where extra petals obscure the stamens by forming a crestlike projection.
I. Fantasy flower with irregular dashes of color on the petals.

Here are some additional terms you may encounter.

Longifolia: leaf is long, narrow, and pointed.
Spoon: leaf has rolled-up margin, particularly toward the stem end.
Tommie Lou foliage: leaves have creamy white edges and speckling that extends more or less into the leaf centers.

Simple Steps for Healthy Growth

Few people want to grow African violets only for their leaves. While the foliage itself is undeniably attractive on a well-grown plant, the beauty most of us seek is in the charming, colorful flowers.

Bringing African violets into flower does not depend on secret knowledge or the proverbial "green thumb." Rather, it involves an understanding of basic and simple cultural needs. However, even under seemingly ideal conditions a plant sometimes will be reluctant to bloom, but this can often be explained by the fact that some African violets are more free with their blooms than are others. Often those that have fewer flowers will compensate by having flowers larger than the usual, while others may bloom profusely for a few months and then rest a few months.

It is difficult to know what a plant's blooming habits are until you have grown it for a while. Give a plant good culture and a fair trial before judging it a shy bloomer. If, however, a plant fails to reward you with flowers after many months of good care, you probably would be happier replacing it with another variety which might be more generous with its blooms; check the Shopping Guide on pages 66-79.

Cultural Guidelines

Although freedom of flowering may vary from variety to variety and, in addition, will depend upon a plant's maturity, there are a number of cultural guidelines which you should follow in order to promote the best possible performance from a plant.

Give Them Light

All plants must have light to survive, and African violets are no exception. While they will grow in a northern exposure, there they will probably have only leaves and no bloom. Generally, African violets need all the light they can get throughout the year except in summer when full sun may be too intense. In spring, fall, and winter, several hours of sun daily are desirable for healthy, blooming plants. It is easy to tell when plants have too much sun: Foliage turns yellow and leaf edges burn. Too little light produces lovely dark green foliage but few, if any, flowers. Therefore, seek the happy medium. A western exposure is good all year for most African violets.

Any window in the home that offers some light (if not totally darkened by trees or buildings) is a potential location for plants. If direct sunlight through a window is diffused somewhat by tree branches, this is an ideal exposure. Light that comes through textured glass is also good. In these situations the light will be enough to keep plants growing but not so bright as to burn leaves. If your African violets are at a south-facing window, keep a thin curtain between the pane of glass and the plants during late spring and summer.

Turn plants a complete 360 degrees every month so that all leaves will receive equal shares of light; an easy way to do this is to give plants a quarter turn each week, always turning in the same direction. Without this turning a plant's symmetry will be spoiled as the leaves constantly receiving the most light will grow larger, longer, and more rapidly than leaves on the plant's shaded side.

Proper light and water *are two important basics of African violet care. Bright light from south window encourages bloom on tabletop plants* (**above**). *Homemade wick pot* (**right**) *provides just the right amount of water without need for constant attention.*

If you have no window space that would provide proper light, you might want to try growing African violets under artifical light. See pages 27-29 for specific directions.

Temperature, Ventilation Come Easily

In the home, African violets will be comfortable if you are. A daytime temperature of 72° to 75° is fine; night temperatures should be around 65°. Excessive heat will harm African violets, so on hot summer days see that your plants occupy the coolest place possible. Likewise, extreme cold will damage plants, so in winter keep them away from windowpanes to avoid temperatures that would go below 55°.

Along with comfortable temperatures, African violets need a well-ventilated growing area. The stagnant air of a closed room only invites ill health and second-rate performance. Direct air currents on plants can, however, be as detrimental as no air movement. The best solution is to provide indirect ventilation—an open window in an adjoining room, or an open window in the same room but far enough from plants that drafts won't reach them. In winter when windows are generally shut, use a small electric fan operating at low speed to keep air moving.

In the zeal of plant collecting it is tempting to gather together as many plants as you can squeeze into a given area. However, just as African violet plants need air circulating in the room, each plant needs air circulating around it. Resist the inclination to crowd plants together and, instead, consider an artificial light garden if you have more plants than the available window space can accommodate.

A dry atmosphere also is detrimental to the health of African violets. Your plants prefer a humidity range from 40 to 60 percent. Ways to provide humidity include misting, using an electric humidifier, grouping plants, and setting plants on water-filled trays of gravel.

Watering Pointers

Frequently the novice African violet grower worries over when and how to water his plants. The simplest guidelines are these: *When* depends on the size of the pot, the weather, and

Top watering *is easy if you have long-spouted watering can to reach under leaves.*

the plant itself. *How*—from top or bottom—depends on your own taste. The one invariable direction is that you must use water which is approximately at room temperature. Cold water has a particularly shocking effect on plants—they may respond by developing leaf spot or by refusing to develop new buds. The easiest way to get room-temperature water without resorting to thermometers is simply to draw the water and let it stand overnight in the same room as the plants before using it.

Bottom watering—putting water in the saucer and letting the soil in the pot soak it up by capillary action—is easy and it avoids the possibility of getting water into a plant's crown. However, top watering—if done carefully so that only the soil is moistened—is not only just as effective, it is sometimes necessary in a bottom-watered collection. When water is taken up into the soil by capillary action, any salts in the water (and the fertilizer salts in the liquid preparations) will gradually accumulate in the soil to the point that eventually they could damage roots. In addition, accumulated salts on the soil surface can cause stem rot. The only way to get rid of these salts before they build up to damaging concentrations is to periodically leach them from the soil by applying water from the top and letting it run through the soil and out the pot's drainage hole.

Fashioning Your Own Wick Pot

Wick pots are a great convenience—they take the worry out of how often to water your African violets and, with a good-size container, they can provide automatic watering for up to 2 weeks when you are away.

You can make your own wick pot from materials found around the house. Even though your homemade product may not be as attractive as the commercial kind (such as the one illustrated on page 14), it will work just as well.

You can make a water reservoir from any one of a number of household items. A ½-pound butter dish, a cheese container, or a refrigerator storage container are adaptable. Squatty containers (having more width than height) are better balanced and more esthetically pleasing than tall containers. Remember that a clear container allows you to see when the reservoir needs refilling.

For a wick, you can improvise with strips of nylon stockings or any absorbent organic fabric, such as rope or thick twine or even strips of your old pajamas.

Or you can buy long-lasting glass wicks at some nurseries and hardware stores.

The soil for the wick-fed pot must be light and fast-draining. To lighten your present mix, add extra perlite or vermiculite.

Though watering is automatic with a wick pot, you should remember some rules. Allow the soil to dry out just a little before you refill the reservoir. Should the soil accidentally get too dry, you'll have to pour a little water on the top of the soil ball after you refill the reservoir.

You can add a liquid or dissolvable powder fertilizer directly to the reservoir water.

It's a good idea to water from the top of the pot once a month to wash away any accumulated salts caused by fertilizer or hard water. To make refilling easy, you may wish to cut a ½-inch hole near the lid's edge so that you can add water to the reservoir without having to remove the plant and the lid.

Wash the reservoir with hot water once a month to prevent algae and mineral residue buildup.

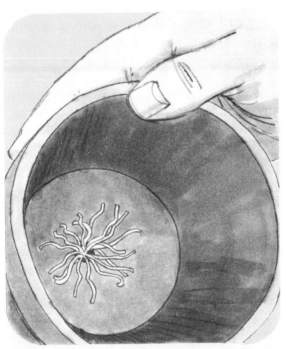

Spread out *enough of unbraided wick to cover bottom of pot; then cover wick with damp soil.*

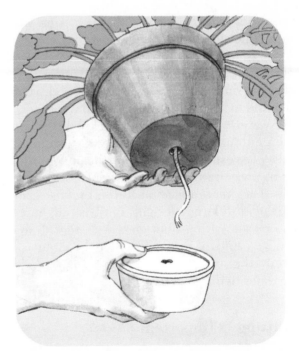

Place dangling end *of wick into water reservoir; fill reservoir and pour some water into soil.*

If you regularly water your African violets from the bottom, a thorough once-a-month top watering should be sufficient.

Watering from the top requires more care and time than bottom watering, as it is difficult—particularly with large mature plants—to hit only the soil and not get water into the plant's crowns. Use a long-spouted watering can (rather than a pitcher, for example) for the greatest accuracy when applying water from the top.

It is difficult to set up rigid watering schedules for all plants. Generally, water African violets in 5 or 6-inch pots about 3 times a week in dull weather. Smaller pots will need water more often. Never allow soil to become soggy; it should be kept evenly moist. When the soil surface begins to feel dry to the touch it is time to apply more water.

Strongly alkaline (hard) water is not good for most plants. If your area has hard water—as in many parts of the Southwest—this condition can be alleviated by a solution of one tablespoon of vinegar in one gallon of water. Use this once a month in place of regular watering and it will help reduce accumulated alkalinity in the potting soil.

The other extreme—water that has been softened artificially with sodium—may be fatal to plants in time. For sodium-treated water there is no corrective measure as there is for hard water. If you can't draw water before it is softened, your recourse is to use rainwater or bottled water.

Self-watering containers and wick-fed pots are convenient innovations for indoor gardeners, and they are especially a boon for the person who must be away from his African violets for days at a time. The different manufacturers of these containers offer different designs, but basically most units operate with a spun glass wick that draws water by capillary action through the drainage hole into the soil. As the water is used, you add more water to the reservoir.

Fertilizing Is Important

As plants grow, their roots deplete the soil of available nutrients. Consequently, to maintain healthy, even growth you will have to fertilize your African violets periodically. The three major elements most needed for healthy

Store-bought *automatic watering device keeps moisture at correct level for healthy plant growth.*

growth—nitrogen, phosphorus, and potassium—are available in commercial fertilizers. The fertilizer labels will state the percentages of these valuable elements—such as 10-10-5, 20-10-10, and so on, with nitrogen listed first and phosphorus and potassium following in that order.

Organic fertilizers such as fish emulsion, animal manure, bone meal, blood meal, or hoof and horn meal can also be used for fertilizing, alternating with a complete balanced commercial formulation.

You can purchase fertilizer that is made specifically for African violets: be sure to read all labels carefully to select a moderate strength fertilizer with a formula of about 10-10-5. Fertilizers with too much nitrogen will give you handsome robust plants, but there will be little bloom.

Commercial fertilizers come in liquid or granular form. The liquids and many granular types are to be mixed with water; some granular or pelletized fertilizers can be applied directly to the soil where regular waterings will dissolve them. Generally, use a little less than the label recommends to avoid any possibility of burning the plants. Fertilize your African violets about once a month throughout the spring, summer, and fall, not at all in the winter. Whenever you fertilize, be sure the soil is moist before you apply the solution.

While fertilizing is intended to benefit plants, it can also be harmful if used at inopportune times. For example, after a plant has had a big burst of flowers, let it rest; don't fertilize it and try to force it back into bloom again right away. And never fertilize sick or newly potted plants.

Pots and Potting Techniques

A few years ago there were perhaps a dozen varieties of containers for plants; today there are hundreds. While African violets can be grown in almost any container, the standard, time-tested clay pots are still best because water evaporates slowly through the material. Many plastic pots perhaps look more attractive, but they will keep soil moist longer than clay pots will, and this prolonged moistness can lead to crown rot if you water too often. Should you decide to use plastic pots, plant your African violets in a soil mixture that is very coarse and porous (see pages 17-18).

Glazed pottery pots are also available but many of these do not have drainage holes through which any excess water can escape. If you try to grow African violets in such drainless pots, you generally end up with soggy soil which eventually means death for the plant. If you seek the decorative effect of the glazed pot and want to use it as it is, slip an African violet in a clay pot into the glazed container rather than potting the plant directly in it. Of course, if you have a drainage hole drilled in the bottom of a glazed pot (most stores which sell glass and nurseries will be able to do this for you), you can plant your African violet directly in it, observing the same precautions you would with plastic containers.

Novelty containers such as strawberry jars also will grow and display African violets well. Most of them have drainage holes; if they do not, you can have holes drilled just as you would for glazed ceramic pots.

Generally, single-crowned African violet plants are intolerant of large containers; the soil that is not occupied by roots can become soggy and sour, a condition which can lead to eventual crown rot. Most African violets seem to bear a better crop of flowers in "tight" pots—pots that are just large enough to accommodate their root system. So use the smallest size pot that will hold the plant and still be in proportion to it. Place seedlings and rooted leaves in 2¼-inch pots. In about nine months shift them to 3-inch pots; when they are 9 inches across, to 4-inch pots; and at 12 inches, to 5-inch pots. Larger, mature specimens (15 inches or more) may require a 6-inch pot. Squatty pots are ideal for the shallow-rooted African violet.

First, be sure to thoroughly clean old pots before you use them again. It's a good idea to immerse them in boiling water for a few minutes to sterilize them; then scour pots to remove dirt and crusted salt deposits. Let new clay pots soak in water for a few hours so they will absorb water and therefore not draw moisture from the soil when you water your newly potted plant. On plastic pots use hot water and a detergent; scrub them carefully to remove all old soil, then let them dry.

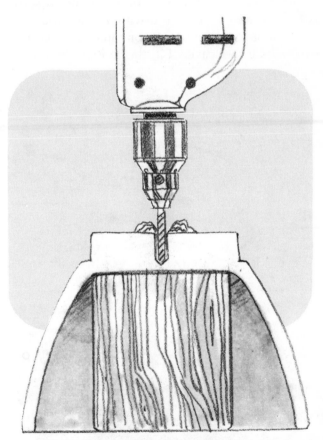

You can drill holes *in some drainless pots. Brace inside of bottom with wood block, then drill.*

To remove a potbound plant from its container, slip your hand under the rosette of leaves (with your palm against the soil surface) and hold the plant's crown between two fingers; then turn the pot upside down and tap it sharply against a table edge. Try to ease the plant from its container; do not pull but rather tease it loose. You should end up with the root ball and soil in the palm of your hand, the plant against the back of your hand (see the illustration below). If it still does not come out, take a knife and run it around the inside of the pot between pot and soil, then repeat the process just described.

Place a curved piece of broken pottery (convex side facing upward) over the new pot's drainage hole before adding new soil. Then put in a mound of your potting soil and center the plant on it. If the plant sits too low in the pot, lift it out and add more soil to bring it up to the proper level; if the plant is too high, take away some soil. After you have the plant positioned, fill in and around with additional potting soil; rap the bottom of the pot sharply on the table to settle the soil, and firm the soil with a blunt stick—or your fingers or thumbs, if you can do this without damaging the leaves. Fill the container with soil

to within half an inch of the pot's rim; this will allow space for water when you top water your plants. Thoroughly soak the newly-potted plant, let it drain, and then resoak the soil. Set the plant in a protected, somewhat shaded area and

Position plant *on mound of potting mix. Fill in and around root ball with additional potting mix.*

Gently firm soil *with your thumbs, fingers, or a blunt stick; then water plant thoroughly, drain, and water again.*

Remove plant *from container by placing palm against soil; invert pot and tap on table edge.*

water only moderately for a few weeks—just keep the soil barely moist. Then move the African violet to its permanent place and follow a regular watering schedule.

If you delay repotting too long, faster growing varieties will form a "trunk" above soil level where old leaves have fallen off. When repotting, bury this trunk up to the lowest leaves, and new roots will form along it (in time, old roots shrivel and die). You also can sever the roots from the trunk and reroot the plant in water.

Soil Should Be Special

When you buy soil for your African violets, feel it; it should be porous, almost fluffy. It should never be heavy or sticky because then when it is wet it will be impervious to air and roots will not be able to grow satisfactorily. Almost all African violets will fare well in the time-tested standard mix for house plants: one third garden loam, one third leaf mold, and one third sand. This is a light mixture that will retain water long enough for health but not so long that it harms roots.

There are, almost literally, as many potting mixtures for African violets as there are African violet growers. A variation of the above mixture is two parts leaf mold or peat moss, and two parts garden loam, mixed with one part vermiculite. To this combination some growers add a handful of sand, some perlite, and a sprinkling of charcoal chips. What you ultimately use depends on what will grow plants best for you. Just remember that soil *must* be light and porous.

No matter what soil you choose, it should be sterilized (or, more properly, pasteurized). Packaged soil mixes come already sterilized. If you buy one of these, look for those especially formulated for African violets. If you use garden soil in a soil preparation you'll have to sterilize it yourself. The oven method is a simple, but smelly, procedure. Mix together the ingredients

Vacation Treatment for Your Violets

What do you do with African violet plants at vacation time? If you are going away only for a few days, most African violets will survive without any special consideration. If you are going to be gone a week or more, perhaps a friend can come in and water them for you. Of course, plants in self-watering containers will get along with no attention.

Should you have to leave your African violets entirely on their own for a few weeks, put them in a bright place (but without direct sun) where temperatures will remain on the cool side of their preferred range. Then moisten soil and cover the plants with polyethylene plastic sheeting, or cover individual plants with plastic bags. This helps to preserve humidity and keep soil moist. Before covering plants with plastic, remove all flowers and buds that are large enough to open while you will be gone. Flowers that decay on leaves in high humidity may provide a breeding ground for fungus spores.

Another vacation treatment for African violets is to put plants in a cardboard box filled with moist sphagnum moss. Pack the plants close together in the moss, but be sure there is adequate ventilation in the growing area. This should keep plants moist as long as the sphagnum stays damp.

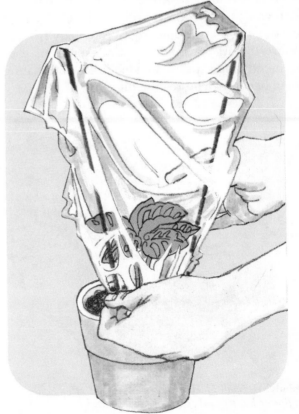

Plastic bag *keeps plant moist enough to be left unattended for short period of time.*

in a large pan; add enough water to saturate the mix, cover it, and bake in an oven at 180° for at least 2 hours. Then cool the mixture and air it for 3 or more days before planting in it, stirring it several times during this period.

Some specially-formulated African violet potting mixtures contain no soil. In these soilless mediums, plants will need fertilizer more often than plants grown in mixes that contain soil—particularly if the soilless preparation drains rapidly and retains little moisture. If you buy plants already potted, ask what kind of mixture they are planted in for an indication of fertilizer and water needs.

If Problems Develop

Like all plants, African violets have their share of possible problems, although in varying degrees. Some growers never see a mite or an aphid; others are not so fortunate. The best advice is still that an ounce of prevention *is* worth a pound of cure. Applied to African violets this means that you should observe your plants: Inspect leaves and stems frequently to catch any trouble before it starts. A mild insect infestation is easy to remedy; once pests get a foothold, eliminating them becomes a more difficult task.

Catch Pests Early

The common plant pests that you may have occasion to eradicate are: aphids, mealybug, thrips, nematodes, soil mealybug, and cyclamen mite. If you catch them before they have a chance to get a foothold, they are easy to eliminate.

Nematodes (root) are soil pests—fine, thread-like, parasitic worms that infest roots, causing the plants to assume a sickly yellow green color and a tired, drooping appearance. For definite evidence of nematodes, remove the ailing plant from its pot and examine its roots; if they show signs of swelling or if the stalk at the soil line is spongy, root-knot nematodes may be at work. *Control:* The best and safest remedy is to discard the infested plant, since the only effective control involves working with nematocides (chemicals which will kill nematodes). These toxic materials, which must be handled with extreme care, have been taken off the market and require a license for use. And, even if you use a nematocide, chances for a plant's recovery are slim. To prevent nematodes, use only sterilized potting soil.

Mites are minute pests, several kinds of which can be troublesome for many different plants. Cyclamen mite probably is the most serious pest of gesneriads, especially dangerous because the

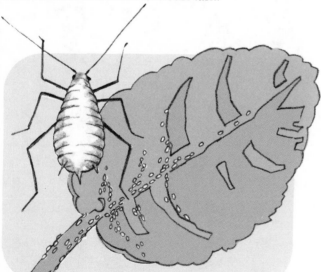

Aphids *are small black or green pests that often collect on flower buds or other soft, new growth.*

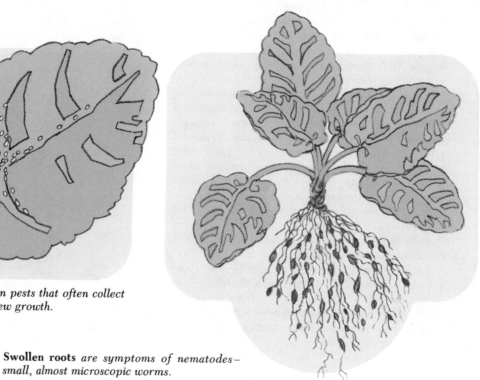

Swollen roots *are symptoms of nematodes— small, almost microscopic worms.*

mites cannot be seen without the aid of a magnifying lens. Only when you see evidence of their damage—distorted, twisted foliage, streaked flowers, and stunted growth—do you know they're there. The first indications usually are in the center of a plant: The crown appears lighter than the rest of the leaves, the small leaves there become grayish or yellow green, and they remain small and twisted. If you notice cobwebs on flowers or leaves and if foliage is at all brown or stippled, then red spider mites are at work. If broad mite attacks a plant, the leaves usually will curl down (if it is cyclamen mite they will curl up). *Control:* First, isolate your mite-infested plants from those which appear to be clean. Then, treat the infested plants with diazinon or malathion. You can use these as sprays or you may immerse the plants in a spray solution (after first covering the soil surface so that soil will not unnecessarily cloud the solution). Especially if you dip the plants, wear protective gloves so that toxic solution does not contact your skin. Usually several treatments, spaced about a week apart, will clean up an infestation.

Aphids are small, soft-bodied insects, usually black or green, that accumulate on new growth and suck out vital plant juices. *Control:* Wash them off daily with lukewarm water; if infestation is severe, use a rotenone or pyrethrum spray, or malathion or diazinon.

Mealybugs—soft, cottony white insects—lodge themselves in leaf axils and on undersides of leaves, occasionally deep in the crown of the plant. They suck vital plant juices and can destroy a plant if not eliminated in time. *Control:* Rub them off the plant with an alcohol-dipped cotton swab, then carefully wash the plant in lukewarm water. Repeat this operation daily until all newly hatched mealybugs are destroyed. Effective materials are malathion and diazinon.

Soil mealybugs are insidious because they do their work underground and can go undetected for a long time. If a plant appears wilted or stunted, soil mealybugs may be at work. They destroy the root tips so that a plant becomes unable to take in water and fertilizers in solution. To be sure, remove the plant from its pot and examine the root ball; if you see grayish white bugs on the surface of the root ball you'll know this is the problem. *Control:* The best control is prevention—plant only in sterilized soil. If you have an infested plant that you must save, soak the soil with a malathion solution.

Thrips are tiny (almost microscopic) slender insects, pale yellow when young and brown when

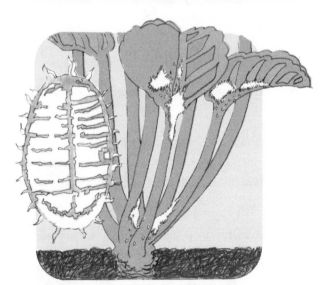

Mealybugs *look like spots of white cotton, usually collect under leaves.*

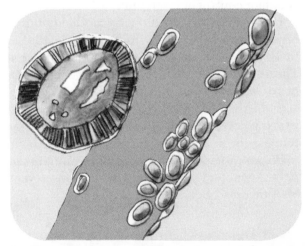

Small tan discs *are actually scale insects, infrequent pests of some gesneriads; usually on stems.*

mature, that move about rapidly when disturbed. They can cause premature bud drop and streaking of flower petals, and a white stippling on leaves. *Control:* The same sprays that control aphids will eradicate an infestation of thrips. Removal of all flowers and buds helps eliminate a primary source of infestation.

Scale is an infrequent offender but may be found occasionally on some gesneriads. It is a small, waxy, flattened disk-shaped insect, usually in some shade of tan to yellow, often accompanied by a black, sticky exudate. *Control:* Remove scale with a toothpick or toothbrush dipped in mild soap (not detergent) and lukewarm water; then wash leaves with clear, lukewarm water. Effective toxic sprays are malathion, diazinon, or systemics.

Pesticides

You will find many insecticides at your local nursery or garden supply center. Some are formulated to kill specific pests (such as mites or aphids); many preparations are made for specific plants such as roses or African violets.

Observation is the best weapon against insects and disease. Any mild infestation usually can be eradicated with home remedies. These include hand picking of insects, washing plants with warm water, or using cotton swabs dipped in alcohol for control of mealybugs or aphids.

However, if insects do get a foothold and you must resort to toxic controls, first use the less toxic poisons such as pyrethrum and rotenone. These are botanical insecticides (derived from plant extracts) that will control aphids, thrips, and mealybugs. For severe insect infestations use diazinon or malathion or one of the systemics; these are the safest of the more highly toxic insecticides for use around humans and pets. Always follow carefully the directions on an insecticide's label.

Most Diseases Can Be Dodged

In contrast to insects—which can invade perfectly healthy collections—most diseases will be avoided if you have your plants in congenial locations and give them regular attention. In fact, only virus infections are beyond your control.

Botrytis blight is a gray mold that turns blooms and buds into mushy, brown tissue. Epidemics develop under cool, moist conditions with high humidity. Most often the fungus enters the plant through dead or dying flowers or leaves, but when conditions are right it will infect live tissue. *Control:* Be sure plants have good air circulation; avoid high humidity and overfertilization with nitrogen. At the first sign of infection, remove dead plant parts and parts attacked by botrytis, then apply a fungicide such as benomyl, captan, or thiram. Isolate infected plants until you are sure the disease is under control.

Ring spot usually appears as yellow rings on the upper leaf surfaces and is generally caused by

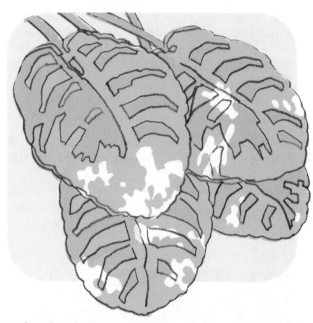

Light-colored rings *or irregular mottling on leaf surfaces indicate ring spot, caused by cold water on leaf.*

cold water coming in contact with soil or foliage. Sunlight on wet leaves also can cause ring spot. *Control:* Use only tepid water when watering your African violets, and keep water off leaf surfaces if they will be exposed to sunlight.

Viruses (such as tobacco mosaic, for example) occasionally attack various gesneriads. Their presence is easy to identify: streaked, distorted leaves, sometimes with irregular yellow spots, on a plant generally lacking in vigor. *Control:* There is no effective cure for virus, so infected plants should be removed from a collection and destroyed.

Crown rot is indicated if a healthy plant suddenly starts wilting. This disease most often gets its start in plants that are erratically watered so that their root environment alternates between desert and bog conditions. *Control:* Avoid overwatering (with the resulting soggy soil) and avoid alternating extremes of wetness and dryness in the potting soil. Also be careful, when watering, to keep water from settling in the crown of the plant. If crown rot develops but has not progressed to the fatal point, repot the plant. First remove it from its container, shake off all soil, and remove dead roots and soft stems; apply sulfur to all areas where you have cut out rotten tissue. Then repot the plant.

Is Poor Culture the Culprit?

While insects can be responsible for the decline of a plant, many times cultural conditions may be at fault, instead. The information in the accompanying chart will help you to determine if pests are at work or if your plants' problems stem from growing conditions.

Words to the Wise . . .

To avoid any problems with African violets, you should observe a few basic rules no matter how foolish they may seem when you have what appears to be a perfectly healthy plant:

• Isolate new plants from your others for one to two months. During this period, observe them closely for the presence of any insects.
• Be wary of introducing plants other than African violets into your collection; they may carry diseases or insects that also will affect African violets. (If you do add other plants—other gesneriads, for example—follow the isolation procedure mentioned above.)
• Plant only in sterilized soil.
• If a plant begins to sulk (if leaves go limp or if spots develop on leaf stems), immediately remove it from the vicinity of your other plants.

Plant Problems

Symptoms	Possible Causes	Remedy
Weak stems, smaller leaves than normal, flowering sparse or not at all	Insufficient light	Move plant to a better lighted window or set up a fluorescent light garden
Leaves have dull brown edges, flowers are smaller than normal	Insufficient humidity	Place pots on trays or plant saucers filled with gravel and water
Soft, rapid growth and lack of flowers	Temperature too high	Move to a room where temperature stays between 65° and 75°.
Growth slow and leaves curl downward	Temperature too low	Move to a room where temperature stays between 65° and 75°.
Leaves become yellow, growth is small, and flowers are smaller than normal	Insufficient fertilizing	Try fertilizing plants twice a month
Leaves dark green but flowers few	Too much fertilizing	Fertilize half as often as usual, and use a fertilizer lower in nitrogen
Leaves drop or flower buds drop off	Sudden temperature change	Move plants to a location not subject to rapid changes
Leaves become brittle, brown	Soil is deficient in nutrients	Repot plant if soil is old, and begin regular fertilizing
Leaves develop brown spots	Plants watered with cold water	Always use room-temperature water
Bleached, tired looking foliage	Too much light	Remove plants from direct sunlight

African Violets Are Easy to Live With

The virtues of African violets as indoor decoration lie in their combination of beauty and versatility. Truly, African violets come close to being an all-purpose decorating item. You will find them used effectively *en masse* at windows, under artificial lights in a sunless part of a room, grouped on plant stands, in terrariums, or simply as cheerful accents on coffee tables, in entry halls, or on well-lighted kitchen counters—to mention only a few possibilities. For an effective mass display (as a table centerpiece, for example), try grouping several pots of blooming African violets in a large, shallow container such as a metal bowl. Or, for eye-level enjoyment, grow a few African violets in hanging baskets or suspended pots. There are even trailing varieties that are especially suited to hanging display—indoors at windows or outdoors (in spring and summer) from porch eaves and rafters.

Unlike many other house plants that eventually may outgrow their allotted spaces, African violets will remain a predictable size and can be easily moved to any suitable location in the home. The only danger is that you may be tempted to grow more than you have room for!

Window Displays Are Naturals

Before the advent of fluorescent lights, a window was the only place where you could grow African violets. Naturally, window displays have always been popular—there, plants are assured of receiving adequate light and they can be viewed easily—and windows continue to be the most frequently used staging for amateur growers with moderate-size collections.

There are many possibilities for shelf arrangements that will hold plants at windows; the choice is largely a matter of personal taste and ingenuity. For standard window sizes you often can buy pre-cut and packaged glass shelves with the necessary brackets to hold them up. If your windows are odd sizes you can still purchase brackets separately and have shelves cut to fit out of ¼-inch plate glass. Shelves of wood are even easier to install because you can do whatever cutting and fitting is necessary. As a rule-of-thumb example, three shelves, each 24 inches long and 8 inches wide, will give you space for about fifteen African violets without crowding. You'll probably want to have each pot sitting in its own saucer; this will protect shelves and windowsills from water stains and will prevent water from dripping off shelves onto plants below.

Where existing window sills are not wide enough for plants but the light is good, you might use portable plant stands, tea carts, or narrow tables placed by the windows to gain space for your potted plants. If you use portable stands or carts you can easily move your blooming African violets from room to room whenever you want a temporary display of color.

Try Hanging Violets

Although you have not nearly as many varieties from which to choose as you do from the lists of the usual rosette-forming plants, there are some African violets which have a trailing growth habit. These are tailor-made for showing off in hanging pots or baskets. But even if you don't have one of the trailing sorts, a large multiple-crowned plant of any of the usual types can put

Greatly adaptable *African violets can grow almost anywhere as long as they receive proper light and temperature. Portable table-top light fixture* (**above**) *brings the charm of these plants to almost anywhere in the home. Brandy snifter* (**right**) *displays delicate miniature.*

on a spectacular show when suspended at eye-level. With nothing close to crowd them, these hanging plants enjoy good air circulation.

Hanging plants can be suspended in two ways: The basket or pot is attached to at least two wires, cords, or chains which are connected to a hook or eye inserted in the ceiling; or, the hanging container is held up by a wall-mounted bracket. The latter can be easily attached to a window frame; then you simply hang the pot from the bracket.

You will find a wide assortment of containers in which you can grow plants for hanging. Some containers are specifically designed for hanging, while others can be adapted easily to this purpose. There are manufactured wire attachments, for example, which will attach to a standard clay pot and allow you to suspend it; even better are the devices which attach to the pot's saucer (you then just set the pot in the saucer) so that watering the hanging plant entails no mess from water dripping onto the floor beneath. Glazed ceramic pots often are especially decorative hanging accents, but for those that have no drainage holes you will want to keep your African violet plants in standard clay pots and slip them inside the glazed ceramic ones.

Inexpensive wire or wire mesh baskets can be used to feature hanging African violets but not without this special preparation: first, line the basket with a layer of sphagnum moss so the potting soil will be contained in the basket. Add the potting soil (and then the plant) only after the sphagnum liner has been firmed in place. You'll probably have to pay more close attention to watering African violets in wire baskets than you would plants in other containers, since the sphagnum liner (rather than the sides of a ceramic or plastic pot) is all that comes between potting soil and air. Unless the floor beneath wire baskets is of a material that is not bothered by water, you'll have to take the baskets down and water them at the sink whenever they need it; otherwise water will drain through the sphagnum and onto the floor below.

African violets in hanging baskets are always on display, which means that grooming is particularly important for these plants.

For plants in side *of basket, push plant's root ball through hole or slit in moss.*

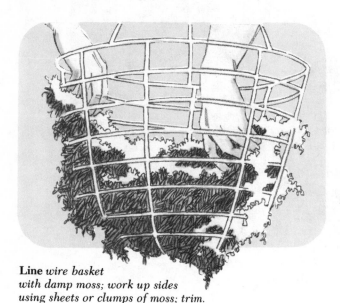

Line *wire basket with damp moss; work up sides using sheets or clumps of moss; trim.*

Set plants *in top of basket as you would in a pot; fill in and around plant with soil up to 1 inch of top.*

Miniature Greenhouses

Miniature greenhouses are what you're giving your African violets when you plant them in glass vessels such as bubble bowls, bottles, brandy snifters, apothecary jars, and the like. And when grown "under glass" the plants almost never suffer from lack of moisture or humidity. With the larger glass bowls, jars, or bottles you can even try your hand at creating miniature landscapes, featuring African violets but including other compatible plants as well. The combination of sparkling glass encasing a robust blooming plant is invariably a showpiece.

Miniature and semi-miniature African violet varieties are ideal choices for growing in glass containers, for even with such congenial moisture and humidity they still will not be likely to outgrow the confines of the glass vessel. In fact, the miniatures may actually grow better in a glass enclosure because the soil moisture will fluctuate much more slowly than it does in the very small pots which miniatures require.

Even if you decide to grow only miniature African violets in this manner, you should choose a glass container that is at least 8 inches across at its widest point. This is about the smallest size that will accommodate miniatures without appearing to cramp them.

With glass bowls, jars, or bottles there will be no drainage holes for water to escape. Therefore, preparation of the potting soil—as well as subsequent watering—will have to be done with special care. Be sure the potting soil is sterilized; either buy a sterilized prepared mixture or prepare your own according to the directions on pages 17-18. Whatever mixture you use, it should be one that will not become soggy and dense. Before planting, first place a 1-inch layer of charcoal and gravel on the bottom; cover this with sphagnum moss; then place at least 3 inches of soil on top. Plant your African violet, carefully firm the potting soil around the plant roots, and water lightly—just enough to provide good contact between potting soil and roots.

Watering is most easily done with a watering can that has a long, slender spout. With this, you can direct the water just onto the soil, keeping glass and plant free of water marks or splashed soil. Remember, you don't want soil to be wet but rather just moderately moist.

Set your garden-in-glass where it will receive good light but never direct sunlight, as sun coming through glass will easily burn plants.

Fertilize only when plants show definite signs that they need it. Obviously you want them to

Three layers *of material make this non-draining glass bowl usable; layers are charcoal, moss, and potting mix.*

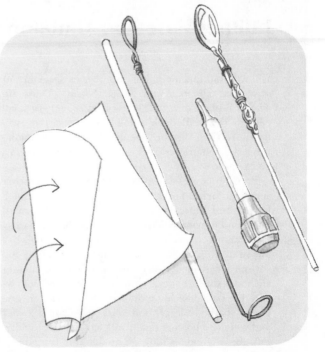

Bottle-potting tools: *from left to right, rolled paper, wooden stick, wire loop, baster, spoon on stick.*

bloom well, but you don't want them to quickly outgrow the limits of their glass enclosure.

Miniature landscapes, using miniature African violets and other small companion plants, can be staged attractively in larger glass containers like aquariums. Here, you can create replicas of natural scenes but in diminutive proportions, making small hills and valleys, using small stones and gravel to imitate natural rock outcroppings and dry stream beds. Some small plants to use with your African violets in these landscapes are: small ferns and palms; mosses, liverworts, and lichens; *Fittonia verschaffeltii; Maranta leuconeura; Pilea involucrata;* and *Soleirolia soleirolii* (baby's tears).

Soil preparation and planting for miniature landscapes is no different from the basic methods just described.

Bottle gardens offer the same cultural and decorative advantages as do gardens in brandy snifters, bubble bowls, and aquariums. The difference is that it is more difficult to plant and maintain bottle gardens simply because of the small opening through which you have to work.

Soil for bottle gardens should be the same as for the other glass-enclosed plantings, and preparation for planting differs in only one respect. You will want to keep the inside walls of the bottle entirely free of soil particles; to do this, make a slender funnel, long enough to reach nearly to the bottom of the bottle, from a sheet of stiff paper. Then pour drainage material and soil through it.

Planting is best done using a length of flexible copper tubing, a pronged wooden stick, or a bent coat hanger—any of which will reach through the neck of the bottle and down to the soil to help position the plant. First, make a hole for the plant's roots in the soil mixture; then carefully ease the plant—roots first—down through the bottle's neck and into the hole, using the stick or tubing as tweezers. When the plant is positioned, use the end of the tubing or stick to tamp the soil down. The necessary tools are illustrated on page 25.

An easier approach to bottle gardening (although results are longer in coming) is to sow African violet seeds directly on the soil in the bottle. Then, as the seeds germinate, thin out the plants until only a few remain. As these come into bloom you may want to remove all but the most attractive specimen.

Lilliput Varieties: Miniature African Violets

You will find that a number of nurseries specialize in or at least offer miniature African violets. These are perfect replicas of regular-size varieties, yet are small enough that a 2½-inch pot is the largest they will need. To the collector, one advantage to the miniatures is that more varieties can be accommodated in a given space.

True miniatures do not get any larger than 8 inches across (6 inches for show) and have relatively small leaves and blossoms. Semi-miniatures are small plants but they have flowers as large as the standards.

Because the small pots miniatures need will dry out so quickly, it often is easier (and wiser) to group several small plants together in a larger container such as a shallow bonsai dish or a clay azalea pot. Be sure the container has a drainage hole. With several plants sharing a larger soil mass, watering is easier and you need not fear that plants will dry out rapidly. Potting soils and planting are no different from directions described on pages 15-18.

If you prefer to keep your miniatures in their individual small containers but want a way to keep soil from drying out quickly, sink several potted miniatures in a large container of sterilized potting soil and keep this soil moist too.

Be cautious of putting miniature African violets in tea cups and other decorative small containers that have no drainage holes, as soggy soil conditions will easily harm plants with such small root systems. For the best results—and an outstanding display for them—try growing your miniatures in small "greenhouses": bubble bowls, jars, decanters, and snifters. This is described on page 25. Surrounded by glass, the plants are protected from drafts and fluctuating temperatures, and the increased humidity within the container will produce healthier plants. Another advantage: moisture condensing inside the glass container helps water the plants.

You'll find a list of popular miniatures and semi-miniatures on pages 76-77.

How to Handle Artificial Light

Artificial light set-ups can brighten the darkest corners of your house—from basements to bookcases, closets to kitchens. Getting the most out of these light set-ups will take experience and a little experimenting. Here are a few guidelines.

The distance you should set your plants from the light depends on two factors: the type of light and the maturity and variety of the plant.

If the light is an ordinary fluorescent tube, you'll need to set your plants closer to the source than if the light is from special growth lamps. Because an incandescent bulb is hotter than a fluorescent tube, it must be set 8 to 10 inches higher above plants.

The maturity of plants also dictates the distance between plants and lamp. The distances we suggest are measured from the top of plants to the light source. If you are setting seedlings under artificial light for their first time, start them at 10 inches to avoid burning them. Then gradually move them up to within 6 to 8 inches. You may set a newly sown tray of seeds as close as 4 inches from the light source (but be careful they don't dry out).

Set mature plants of dark-leaved, dark-flowered, and double-flowered varieties 6 to 8 inches from ordinary white tubes and 8 to 10 inches from special growth lamps. Arrange varieties that require less light—such as plants with variegated or girl-type foliage or white or pink flowers—around the edges of the lamps where the light is less intense. Place miniatures on inverted pots so they stand about 5 inches from the light source.

The amount of time you leave the lights on each day can also vary. An accepted minimum exposure is 10 hours, but to avoid overheating during very warm days, you can reduce time to 8 hours. On normal days, start your plants at the 10 hour minimum, gradually working them up to 12, 14, or even 16 hours a day to determine what works best.

Table-top *fluorescent fixture converts any flat surface into a growing area. An advantage of this type of unit: it can be moved easily to a new location. Strap iron frame holds two fluorescent tubes.*

Gardening by Artificial Light

Your African violet collection need not be limited by the availability of well-lighted window space. You can have thriving plants almost anywhere in your home if you use artificial light to illuminate a growing area. African violets are among the most rewarding plants to grow under artificial light. First of all, their light requirements are not excessive; two 40-watt fluorescent tubes, going for 12 hours a day, will accommodate 9 to 12 plants. Furthermore, African violets are neutral day-length plants—that is, they do not require a specific number of hours of darkness or of light to bloom, but will do so instead under a wide range of day lengths. Since you will not be restricted to space at or near windows, the artificial-light growing area can be anywhere in the house: an unused book shelf, a room divider planter, part of the garage, a basement, a space over the kitchen counter—any spot that would be improved by growing plants.

All plants grown under artificial light respond best to the light quality that most closely approximates natural light. From sunlight, plants use chiefly the red and blue radiant energy from opposite ends of the light spectrum—and about twice as much red light as blue. Red light stimulates vegetative growth; blue light regulates the respiration.

One way to provide the essential light for growth is to use a combination of ordinary natural-white and daylight-type fluorescent lights. Allow 15 to 20 watts of light for each square foot of growing area—so that two 40-watt lamps, for example, are all you would need for a 4-foot square area such as a 1 by 4-foot shelf.

Incandescent lights usually are not strong enough in the red or blue areas of the light spectrum, they generate too much heat for tender plant leaves, and they deliver only about a third as much light for the same amount of electricity as do fluorescent lights. However, some growers feel that using an incandescent bulb of low wattage does aid plant growth. If you try this, use one 8-watt incandescent bulb for each 40-watt fluorescent tube, and place it at least 18 inches above plants to forestall any damage from the heat the bulbs emit.

Several manufacturers of electric lights and fixtures have developed fluorescent tubes designed especially for growing plants indoors. Each tube combines a high intensity of light at both the red and blue ends of the light spectrum. Some growers use these tubes exclusively, while others use them in combination with the standard fluorescent tubes. These special tubes are available in standard fluorescent lamp sizes from 24 inches to 96 inches long and will fit into ordinary fluorescent fixtures.

When you purchase a fluorescent light unit you probably will have a choice of preheat tubes or rapid start types. Preheat tubes will have a longer life than the rapid start, and they also are less expensive. Rapid start tubes occasionally balk where the humidity is high.

No matter which type of fluorescent tube you choose, you will also need a reflector. This is a canopy which throws light back onto the plants. Most fluorescent light units come with reflectors attached.

The lifetime of a fluorescent tube varies according to its use. Also, the number of times that lights are turned on and off will affect their life span. It is a good practice to replace the tubes about every 6 months, before their output begins to decline appreciably. When black rings form at the ends of regular fluorescent tubes this indicates the time to replace them.

Cultural Tips

Growing African violets under fluorescent lights is in some ways easier than growing them in natural light, the chief advantage being that you

Humidity trays *with small pebbles that hold pot so water never touches soil or plant roots.*

have greater control over their environment. Keep in mind, though, the following points as you plan and care for your illuminated garden.

Placement of plants. Dark foliage African violets need more light than do the lighter green and variegated sorts. Under standard white fluorescent lamps, place dark foliage varieties 6 to 8 inches below the tubes and directly under them; under tubes especially made for growing plants, the distance from the light source should be 8 to 10 inches—with placement still directly under the tubes. Varieties with light green or variegated leaves can be placed at the ends of the tubes and at the outer edges of the illuminated area where the light is less intense.

Too much light will cause plants to become unnaturally compact—bunched and tightened in the centers—and sometimes leaves will turn gray. With variegated varieties, too much light turns foliage solid green. Observe carefully the performance of your plants to determine if they are receiving too much or not enough light, then shift their positions accordingly.

Time and temperature. In general, African violets need 10 to 12 hours daily of artificial light. To this rule, however, there are exceptions: Under the special lights for plants they will need only 8 to 10 hours a day; and in very hot weather the plants will perform better if you reduce the hours of illumination to about 8. It is helpful to install an inexpensive automatic timer to run lights on and off on a regular schedule. These are

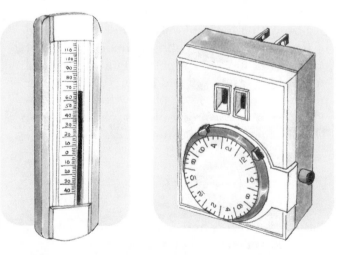

Thermometer and timer *are convenient devices for those who grow African violets under artificial light.*

particularly convenient whenever you have to leave your African violets unattended for a period of time.

Just as for African violets growing in natural light, plants under fluorescent lights need a lower nighttime temperature in order to put on their best performance. For example, if daytime temperature is around 72° then night temperatures should be in the low 60's. Allow the temperature to go down gradually, as an abrupt change would be far more detrimental than no change at all. In most homes, the nighttime temperature is naturally lower than that during the day, so you should need no special apparatus to control the change. However, if your plants are growing in a basement, garage, or other area not usually heated, then you will have to pay special attention to temperature changes.

General care. African violets which grow at or near windows are still somewhat subject to the caprices of weather even though they are indoors. On cloudy days, when light intensity is reduced, plants grow less and transpire less; this reduces their need, on those days, for both water and nutrients. Under artificial lights, on the other hand, your African violets will grow at a fairly constant rate every day, increasing their water and nutrient need and requiring both on a more regular schedule. You will have to check your plants to determine how often they need water (and this still will depend upon the size of the pot and whether it is porous or non-porous). But whatever your watering schedule is, you can use a soluble African violet fertilizer about every week to 10 days throughout the year.

Finally, remember that ventilation and air circulation may assume even greater importance if you have your fluorescent light garden in an enclosed or windowless area where outside air currents (or just the movement of people) won't be available to keep air gently moving around plants. In such situations a small electric fan (but aimed *away* from the plants) running at low speed should keep the atmosphere from becoming stagnant. And along with this goes the same caution that applies to African violets in daylight locations: Don't crowd plants too closely together. If you find you have too many plants for one fluorescent light setup, then start another light garden to handle them.

Propagation–Ways to Increase Your Collection

That nature is a versatile performer is aptly demonstrated by the many ways in which African violets can be propagated. Few plants are less trouble to increase; even the novice African violet grower can raise new plants easily. The simplest method is to root leaves in water; it takes only a second to cut the leaf and put it into water—you need no special equipment. You can also divide multiple-crowned plants by separating the rosettes of leaves and planting each separately, and you can start new plants from suckers—the new shoots which grow from below the crown of a single-crowned plant. And, of course, you can start more plants by rooting leaves in your favorite potting mix, vermiculite, perlite, or other special rooting medium.

If you are slightly more ambitious and want lots of plants, you can sow seed and grow the seedlings on to blooming size. Sooner or later many African violet enthusiasts will want to propagate their very own African violets by hybridizing specific plants in their collection. Perhaps your seedlings will not surpass varieties already named, but each will be different (even if only slightly so) and you will have the satisfaction of knowing that these are your very own plants.

Divide to Multiply

Many people increase their African violet collection without consciously planning to do so. Eventually a plant forms several crowns and gets too large for its container—so they pull off a crown and plant it separately. This is known as division. It takes only a few minutes.

For best results, let the potting soil dry out somewhat before you attempt to divide your plant. Then remove it from the pot and study the plant's spread. With a multiple-crowned plant you will see separate clumps of leaves. Gently but firmly pull these sections apart, making sure to get roots with each division so the separated plants can re-establish themselves quickly. Put the divisions in 3-inch pots with fresh potting soil and water plants only moderately for the first few weeks. Keep the new divisions out of direct sunlight but in a bright place.

Frequently you will see fresh growth emerging below the crowns along the main "trunk." These are referred to as *suckers* and are another source of new plants. (Allowed to grow, they would be responsible for the multiple crowns in a multiple-crowned plant.) When they are large enough to handle, cut them from the main plant with a sharp, sterile knife. Rub the cut surfaces—both on the sucker and the mother plant—with a fungicide. Then dust the cut end of the sucker with a rooting hormone and plant each sucker in a 3-inch pot containing an equal mixture of potting soil and either vermiculite or perlite. Keep the newly planted suckers somewhat dry and in a bright place for a few weeks. Then begin regular watering.

Plants from Leaves

Raising new plants from leaves is one of nature's great conveniences, and it is fascinating to try. Select medium-size leaves, mature but not old, and remove them from the parent plant with 1 to

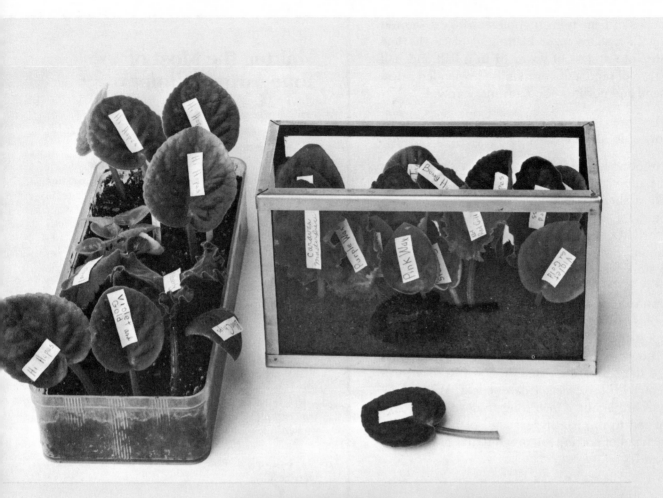

Easily propagated *in so many ways, African violets soon give you many plants. Leaf cuttings* (**above**) *provide most popular method of increase. Seed pod is beginning to swell on hand-pollinated flower* (**right**), *will ripen in 6 to 9 months.*

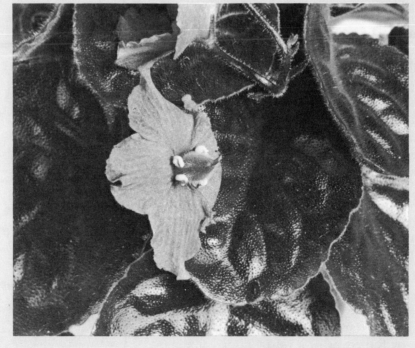

2 inches of leaf stems (petioles). Make a slanted cut with a sharp razor blade and place the leaf stems into a glass of water or in a half and half mixture of sand and vermiculite (expanded mica) or sand and perlite—or in ordinary gravel.

Rooting in Water

For rooting leaves in water, fill a glass with water and secure a piece of aluminum foil over the top. Make a slit in the foil and insert the leaf deep enough for its stem to be in water. Put the glass in a bright but not sunny window; roots will form in about 2 weeks to a month. Plant the rooted leaf stem when new plantlets are about an inch long.

You can also root leaves in water in a bowl of pebbles. Just fill the dish with small stones to support the leaf stems and keep enough water in the bowl to keep stem ends moist. In a little more than a month a small green leaf may push out at the base of each parent leaf. When new leaves are about 1 inch long remove them (still attached to the parent leaf) and plant them in a 3-inch pot of potting soil or a mixture of vermiculite and sand.

Rooting in Soil

Another way of rooting leaves is to put them directly into an African violet potting soil or a potting soil and vermiculite mixture (about an equal percentage of each) or even vermiculite alone. The container for your rooting medium can be anything from a flower pot to a plastic or glass refrigerator container. Insert the leaf stems in the soil mixture just deep enough for them to be propped up but not so deep that they rest on it, as leaves may decay if they remain in prolonged contact with the soil. Toothpicks will help prop up heavy leaves.

At this point you have a choice of two methods: covered or uncovered. If you cover your newly planted leaves with glass or plastic you are giving them a miniature greenhouse environment which will assure them of not drying out during the rooting period. A glass jar, a plastic bag, or the cover of a refrigerator container can be used. If you see excess moisture collecting on the sides of the covering, remove the

Making the Most of Your African Violets

It's easy to propagate African violets in four different ways: leaf cuttings, suckers, divisions, and seeds.

● Leaf cuttings are the most popular propagating method. A leaf can be set in a glass of water or in various rooting mixes (page 32). If you start your leaves in water, transplant them to a rooting mix when the roots are ¼ to ½ inch long. It's possible to grow two "crops" of plants from one leaf: very carefully remove the first set of young plants from the leaf; then replace the leaf into the rooting mix.

● You can remove suckers (the little side shoots near the base of the plant) for propagating when their larger leaves are 2 or 3 inches long (see page 44). Insert suckers into a rooting mix such as that suggested for leaf cuttings.

● If left on the plant, suckers result in a multiple-crowned plant that can be divided into smaller plants (shown below).

● Growing African violets from seed is discussed on page 33.

Separating multiple crowns (divisions) *gives you plants to place in 3-inch pots.*

Rooting leaves in water *is simple, gives you quick results.*

To keep mix moist, *set small, plugged clay pot into mix, fill with water.*

Several new plants *form at base of leaf stalks after 4 to 6 weeks.*

cover for a few hours. In most cases you will not have to water the leaves under cover; natural condensation should supply enough moisture. In uncovered containers you will have to check periodically to be sure the soil does not dry out.

Place the newly planted leaves in a bright location but out of direct sunlight. Keep the propagating mixture slightly moist but never soggy or the leaf stems may rot. About every 10 days, apply a very weak solution of a soluble African violet fertilizer.

Most varieties will root and form new plants in a month to 6 weeks after planting the leaves; some, however, may be more stubborn to start. As long as the leaf stays green and healthy looking, don't despair. After about 4 to 6 months plants will be ready for individual pots.

Keep a vigilant eye out for any rotting leaves. If one leaf cutting in a container of many shows any signs of rot (gray mold or blackening), dispose of it and transfer the other leaves to a clean container with new propagating mix. If plantlets have formed on a leaf that is beginning to rot and they are well along (3 months or more), carefully cut the leaf stem just above the soil surface and discard the leaf.

After the young plantlets are potted on their own, you can discard the mother leaf, or, if you want more new plants, you can reinsert the mother leaf into new potting medium. A second "crop" of plantlets is possible from the same leaf. Remove the first set of plantlets carefully. If you had a good length of leaf stem to begin with, you can cut the original leaf off at the soil level and reinsert the remaining portion of the stem.

Growing from Seed

Today, fine strains of African violet seeds are sold by a number of commercial African violet growers. Although most of the seedlings you raise will not surpass (or, perhaps, even equal) the finest named varieties, the fascination of raising African violets from seed is that no two plants will be exactly alike. Raising mature plants from seed takes no longer than from leaves, but the time span from seed to blooming plant depends on the parent varieties and on the growing conditions you provide for the seedlings.

There are many soil mixtures for seed sowing that you could use, and African violet growers are continually experimenting with new formulas. Actually, if you are in a hurry, the simplest seed starting medium is vermiculite alone. Or, you can use one part milled sphagnum moss and two parts each of perlite and vermiculite. Whatever starting medium you choose, be sure that the mixture has good water holding capacity and yet is light and will drain well. Too much moisture will encourage various fungi which will rot the seeds or young seedlings; use only sterilized soil to minimize this danger.

For easy seed sowing use a shallow flowerpot (such as what is called a bulb pan) and cover it with a sheet of plastic or glass. The cover helps keep the seeds evenly moist, a condition which is essential for good germination. In preparation for seed sowing, just fill the pot with the soil mixture and gently pat it level with your hands.

Scatter the seeds lightly over the prepared soil bed in the dish or pot. Then set a sheet of glass or plastic on the pot and put the pot in a warm (75° to 80°), bright place. If you are growing the seedlings under artificial light, set the plants 3 to 4 inches from the lamps. Germination will begin in about 2 weeks, although this varies somewhat depending on the parent varieties.

Keep the starting mixture barely damp but never really moist. If moisture condenses on the glass, remove the cover for a few hours. When you water, do it with a fine mist which will not disturb the soil surface and wash the seeds out of place. When you actually see green leaves poking through the medium, start watering the seedlings about once a week with a very weak solution of a mild African violet fertilizer and reduce temperatures to around 70°.

During the germination period and young seedling stage, carefully watch the new plants for any signs of damping off. This is a rot which is caused by various fungi that flourish where soil is too wet and air circulation is poor. If you see a cobwebby growth or a gray mold on the soil surface, or if the young plants begin rotting at the soil level, drench the soil with a fungicide solution or dust seedlings with captan.

When the new seedlings each have a few leaves and are about ½-inch tall, transplant each one into a 2¼-inch pot filled with a mixture of

Growing African Violets from Seed

An easy way to increase your African violet collection is to grow them from seed. It's the easiest way to produce large numbers of blooming-size plants in short order. In fact, you can have hundreds of blooming plants from a single seed packet or healthy seed pod in the same amount of time it would take from many leaf cuttings.

You can purchase seed from African violet seed dealers (see page 66) or you can develop your own seeds (see page 36). Sow purchased seeds immediately upon arrival but wait 2 to 3 weeks for sowing seeds from a ripe seed pod after you remove it from the plant.

Seeds can be sown in any number of containers: a shallow pot, a square mason jar (as illustrated), an

Sprinkle seed *slowly onto germinating mix; here spoon is used to sow seed in mason jar.*

Seedlings may appear *as soon as 2 weeks after planting seeds; here seeds were sown in clay pot.*

aquarium, or any other container that can hold rooting medium.

Germination usually takes 2 to 4 weeks but it can take longer. Do not discard the seed tray if nothing has happened within this time—plants may take several months before emerging, and the possibility of producing a prize-winning flower from a late germinator is worth the extra wait.

Transplant *when seedlings are ½ inch tall; you can use a notched plant label for this.*

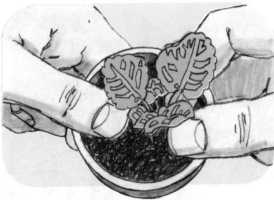

Move larger seedlings *to 2¼-inch pots; use regular potting mix with extra perlite or vermiculite.*

half the seed-starting medium and half your usual African violet potting soil. Try to move all plants with a tiny ball of the soil in which they have germinated clinging to their roots. Push a toothpick or nail file into the soil below a seedling; lift it out gently, and pot each one in individual containers.

Set the newly transplanted seedlings where they will receive good light but no direct sun. After they are established they will enjoy the same amount of sunlight as mature plants do (see pages 10-12). A few weeks after transplanting (about 4 to 6 weeks after the seeds germinate) you can give the seedlings a weak fertilizer solution and put them on the same fertilizing schedule as your other African violets.

If you've noticed that some seeds have not germinated after 2 or 3 weeks (or even a few months), do not dispose of the ungerminated seeds. It's quite possible for some seeds to take up to several months to germinate and finally produce tiny seedlings. And, the late starters often produce better plants.

In 6 to 12 months you can expect the first flowers from your seedling plants. This is an exciting moment. It is now that you can examine your flowers to see if your efforts have been rewarded. If you feel your new plant is promising, you may wish to register it. New varieties usually have improved flower size or color or a new type of foliage. If you do decide your plant has some unique qualities, write to: Registrar, AVSA, Inc., Mrs. Fred Tretter, 4988 Schollmeyer Avenue, St. Louis, MO 63109.

Make Your Own Hybrids

The idea of growing your own African violets from seed is an exciting challenge because no two seedlings will be exactly alike. Directions for sowing seed and handling the seedlings you will find on pages 33-35. At first you probably will try this with seeds you purchase from a commercial African violet grower; but once you raise a few seedlings and become fascinated by the foliage types and flower colors that appear, it is almost inevitable that you will want to make your own hybrid crosses with some particular goals in mind. If your intention is to raise seedlings which will compare favorably with new named varieties, you will have to exercise ruthless selection: Most of your seedlings will be attractive enough for you (or your friends) to grow for indoor color, but few will be really outstanding. But consider what a thrilling experience it would be if you were the first to develop a true red or yellow flower that hybridizers are seeking.

Techniques of Hybridizing

Each African violet blossom contains the necessary male and female elements to make a cross, and these are easily seen by the naked eye. The two small yellow sacs (called *anthers*) in the center of the flower contain the dustlike pollen. The small spike that projects from the flower's center and looks like an insect's antenna is the *pistil.* The slightly enlarged tip of the pistil is the *stigma;* at the other end of the pistil (and beneath the flower) is the *ovary* which will become the seed capsule when fertilized by placing pollen on the stigma.

The best time for pollination is when the flower appears mature (although even when the flower falls off, both pollen and stigma usually are still ripe for fertilization). At this time the stigma becomes slightly sticky, enabling it to hold the pollen. To cross two flowers you must transfer the pollen from the anther of one to the stigma of another; there are several ways you can do this—it is only a matter of using whichever method seems easiest. If you cut a tiny section in an anther and let the pollen fall on your thumbnail, then you can place this pollen on a stigma of your chosen seed parent. Another simple way is to take an anther from a flower (even one that has just fallen off), slit open the pollen sac with a needle, then gently pinch the sac to open it wider and apply the opening to the sticky stigma of the seed parent. A small artists' paintbrush also can be used to transfer pollen to a stigma. During the middle of the day when the air temperature is warm is the best time for making crosses.

After you make a cross you may want to attach a small tag listing the names of each parent to the stem below the pollinated flower. Customarily the seed parent is listed first followed by an "X" and then the name of the pollen parent.

Within a week—if the cross is successful—you will see the seed capsule beginning to grow. As it continues to develop it will protrude more and more from the green calyx which once clasped the base of the flower. It takes anywhere from 6 to 9 months for a seed capsule to ripen; during this time the stem beneath the developing capsule may turn or twist at an angle. Spring is the best time to pollinate the capsules.

The seeds are ripe when the stem and seed capsule turn brown and start to shrivel. When

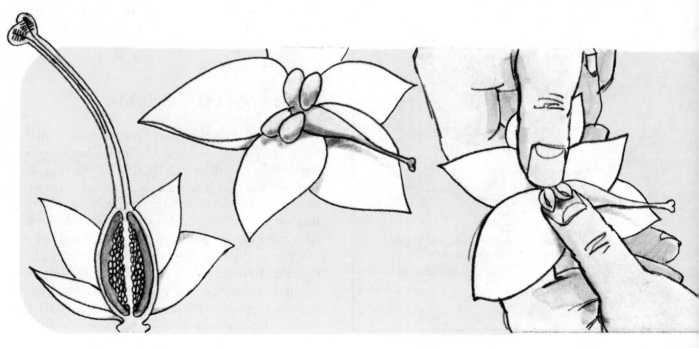

this happens, remove the capsule and put it in an open dish to dry (small jar lids are excellent for this purpose). Be sure to keep different crosses in separate drying dishes so the seeds will not become mixed. Set the dishes in a warm, bright spot and leave them uncovered. Many growers allow seeds to dry for about a month, but you can plant them right after harvesting or as much as a year later.

Occasionally, an apparently healthy seed capsule will turn brown and drop off long before you think it should. Don't throw it away, but instead save it and plant the seeds anyway—some of them may be fertile.

Which Seedlings to Cross?

When your African violet seedlings bloom, you may discover some with colors, form, or leaf types that you would like to keep and use in additional hybridizing. Especially if you have particular goals in mind, it will pay you in terms of time and space saved to have a passing knowledge of basic genetics.

Traits are passed from generation to generation in very complex patterns. When two plants are crossed, each seed that results carries a different combination of characters derived from both parents. Some of the parent characteristics will be expressed more often in the seedlings than will other traits. Those that predominate

are called *dominant*, the others are known as *recessive*. Some of the transmitted characteristics—such as flower color and leaf shape—will be easy to recognize in the seedlings; but others will be so subtle that only an experienced eye would notice them.

It is those unseen differences which often can provide the greatest excitement for you if you cross together two seedlings from the same parents. In *their* offspring—the second generation from your original cross—you may achieve the combinations of characteristics you were striving for, as the dominant and recessive traits sort themselves out to appear in arrangements that differ from their parents and grandparents.

Because most named African violet varieties are so many generations away from the wild species, you often have no way of knowing what recessive characters are carried by the parent plants. For example, if you cross a white flower with a red one thinking to produce a pink-flowered seedling, you may get pink in the first generation but you are just as likely to get red, purple, white, blue, orchid, or lavender—depending upon the genetic backgrounds of the two parent plants. To achieve the pink color you wanted you might have to grow several generations of seedlings. If you are using blue-flowered and/or plain-leafed varieties in your crosses, remember that these two characteristics are dominant over their possible alternatives.

Mechanics of hybridizing: *Cross section of ovary* (**far left**) *shows immature seeds. In illustration* **second from left,** *pistil appears to the right of two anthers. Press pollen onto thumbnail from slit anther sacs* (**third illustration**); *then transfer to stigma (top of pistil above ovary). Developing seed capsules* (**left**) *show how ovary swells as seed matures.*

When It's Show Time for African Violets

T o anyone who becomes fascinated with African violets there comes a time when he will want to attend an African violet show. There, under one roof, can be observed countless varieties that have been groomed and preened to present the best appearance possible for each plant. This allows the showgoer to make reasonably accurate comparative evaluations of the varieties on exhibit. But while viewing the plants, comparing varieties, and generally soaking up the beauty of all those nearly flawless specimens, you are likely to respond to a powerful but unspoken challenge: to try to develop some of your own African violets into show plants. It is difficult to describe the immense satisfaction of producing a specimen worthy of entering in a show—even if your plant doesn't come away with an award ribbon.

The spirit of friendly competition generated by a show does more than just bring forth displays of superbly grown plants. Perhaps more important is that shows bring together fellow hobbyists where they can share experiences and see new developments, and these shows invariably lure newcomers into the ranks of African violet growing.

If you decide you want to try exhibiting your own African violet plants, find out the dates of the next show you could enter. This will let you know exactly how much time you have to get your plants into first class show condition. The points on which a plant is judged are listed on page 40. Remember, even though your potential show specimens may fall short of perfection, there are some "tricks of the trade" you can employ in the weeks before show time to correct what would be judged as faults. See pages 42-44 for these, and start working on your plants as soon as you know when the next show will be held.

It is important to have a copy of the schedule long before the date of the show. This will give you specific information as to classes in which your plants may be entered. The sample schedule on page 41 shows classes that may be included. Schedules will vary according to each show. The schedule should include categories suitable to the club members who will exhibit. Be sure you carefully read the rules and understand them. Otherwise, your entries might be disqualified from competition.

What Makes a Show Plant

In order to produce a specimen African violet that has a chance of competing successfully in a show, you will need to know what qualities of a plant are judged and how important each one is in the overall evaluation. Five aspects of a plant are considered in the judging, and each of the five has a maximum number of points assigned to it. When added together the points total 100—which would indicate a perfect show specimen.

The basic ribbons awarded at shows are for first, second, and third places, and honorable mention. The awarding of these is determined by the total number of points a plant scores during the judging. For a blue (first place) ribbon a plant needs 90–100 points; second place (red ribbon) plants must score 80–89 points; white (third place) ribbons go to specimens in the 70–79 point range.

Congregation *of nearly perfect African violets graces a show table* (**above**). *An award-winning plant* (**right**) *features exceptionally fine, overlapping foliage.*

FIRST PLACE

AVSA Scale of Points for Judging Specimen Plants

Here is the point scale used by the African Violet Society of America and which is used in all shows which follow their rules.

Scale of Points	
Leaf pattern or form (symmetry of plant)	30 points
Floriferousness (quantity of fresh blooms according to variety)	25 points
Condition (cultural perfection)	20 points
Size and type of blossom	15 points
Color (according to variety)	10 points
Total	**100 points**

Symmetry (30 points). Plant symmetry is what the judges will look for first. A perfectly symmetrical plant will have its leaves distributed evenly in a circle—like the spokes of a bicycle wheel—arising from the plant's center. This is the most difficult quality to perfect since you often have to train your plants carefully (and handle them even more carefully) to achieve a perfectly even distribution of leaves. Not all African violets can conform to one standard in this category—some are naturally more compact than others, some naturally grow flat, while others may tend to present a more rounded outline because newer leaves grow upward at an angle from the plant's crown—but the even spacing of leaves should be possible even though growth habits vary from variety to variety.

Floriferousness (25 points). Although plentiful bloom is the objective, it is not always the plant with the most flowers that will score the most points. Rather, the amount of bloom is judged according to variety—some are less free-flowering than others and so have to be scored according to the amount of bloom normal for the variety. The 'Supreme' varieties, for example, typically produce fewer flowers than many other kinds but compensate by having larger-than-normal blooms.

Condition (20 points). A perfectly symmetrical specimen smothered in flowers still can fail to make it to the award table if it shows evidence of careless culture or grooming. Except for varieties with naturally variegated foliage, leaves should be evenly green. Any brown, dead leaf edges, sunbleached or insect damaged leaves will take away points. Poor grooming also will do the same, as points will be deducted for dusty or dead leaves, dead flowers, and visible insects. Points will also be deducted if a sucker has not been completely removed.

Size and type of blossom (15 points). The judges follow the same guidelines here as they do when evaluating the amount of bloom: Some varieties naturally produce larger flowers than others. Therefore, bloom size is judged according to what size flower a variety is expected to produce.

Color (10 points). Cultural conditions—such as the amount and intensity of light a plant receives, the soil it grows in, the type of water you give to it—all influence somewhat the color of flowers. Not that differences in conditions will give you white flowers instead of pink. But the intensity of colors can vary, so that a plant of a particular variety that is showing washed-out color will not score as highly as a plant of the same variety which exhibits blooms of a more "normal" shade.

Training and Grooming

The most important training methods are those which are directed toward making a plant symmetrical. Ideally, this training should begin when the plant is small, so that your training more often will be proper guidance rather than correction.

Begin by placing the young plant exactly in the center of its pot; a symmetrical specimen that is growing off center in its container will lose points at judging time. Then, be sure to turn the plant frequently—as often as once a day would not be too much, but once a week should be the absolute minimum. Turning insures that all leaves on all sides of the plant receive approximately equal light, preventing a tendency to grow lopsided which happens if one side of a plant is more constantly exposed to light than the other.

Sample Show Schedule

Although not all African violet shows will offer all these categories (and some shows may have additional specialty classes), this is a representative "complete" schedule which allows for all possible flower colors and forms.

SECTION 1
Single blossom specimen plants, standard types
Class: 1. Pinks
2. Whites
3. Orchids and lavenders
4. Purples and dark blues
5. Medium and light blues
6. Reds and wines
7. Bicolors, multicolors, Genevas, variegated blossoms

SECTION 2
Double blossom specimen plants, standard types
Class: 8. Pinks
9. Whites
10. Orchids and lavenders
11. Purples and dark blues
12. Medium and light blues
13. Reds and wines
14. Bicolors, multicolors, Genevas, variegated blossoms

SECTION 3
Single blossom specimen plants, Supreme types
Class: 15. Pinks
16. Whites
17. Orchids and reds
18. Purples and blues
19. Bicolors, multicolors, Genevas, variegated blossoms

SECTION 4
Double blossom specimen plants, Supreme types
Class: 20. Pinks
21. Whites
22. Orchids and reds
23. Purples and blues
24. Bicolors, multicolors, Genevas, variegated blossoms

SECTION 5
All specimen plants with variegated foliage, single and double blossoms, standard and Supreme types
Class: 25. Pinks
26. Whites
27. Orchids and lavenders
28. Purples and dark blues
29. Medium and light blues
30. Reds and wines
31. Bicolors, multicolors, Genevas, variegated blossoms

SECTION 6
Miniature and semi-miniature specimen plants, single and double blossoms, green and variegated foliage
Class: 32. Pinks
33. Whites
34. Orchids and lavenders
35. Purples and dark blues
36. Medium and light blues
37. Reds and wines
38. Bicolors, multicolors, Genevas, variegated blossoms

SECTION 7
Original Armacost & Royston hybrids
Class: 39. One plant of each of the ten original hybrids (see page 6 for list of these); each plant must score 85 points or more.

SECTION 8
Seedlings and mutations
Class: 40. Mutations and sports
41. Seedlings

SECTION 9
Specimen plants of species and trailing types
Class: 42. African violet species
43. Trailing hybrids

SECTION 10
Specimen gesneriad plants other than African violets
Class: 44. Columnea
45. Episcia
46. Gloxinia
47. Any other gesneriad
48. Miniature gesneriads

SECTION 11
Terrariums
Class: 49. Gardens under glass, featuring all live plants with African violets predominating and in bloom.

If, as the leaves grow out, they become un-evenly spaced, or if you should accidentally break off a leaf, you still can restore even spacing. Place toothpicks or other small sticks into the soil and against the leaf stalk on the side *away* from the gap you are trying to fill. Gradually move the position of the picks toward the gap—the leaves will adjust to each new position after a few days. To achieve absolutely equal spacing you sometimes may have to shift each leaf's position slightly; always it is the leaves on either side of the gap which will need the most shifting.

Another symmetry problem arises when one or two leaves fail to lie in the same plane as the others in the rosette. When you encounter one of these individualists that sticks out above the rest of the leaves, bring it back into line by looping a hairpin or bent piece of wire over the leaf stalk and inserting the ends into the soil so that the leaf is pulled down into position. After a while you can remove the wire and the leaf should stay in place.

Carefully pinch or break off suckers before they grow so large that they begin to interfere with the plant's symmetry.

A personal pre-show schedule for training your plants, although no guarantee of a blue-ribbon winner, can help you produce a fine blooming plant in time for a local show.

About 10 weeks before the show, select the plants you wish to exhibit. It's a good idea to include a few extra plants just in case some of your favorites do not cooperate by show time. Make sure all the plants are symmetrical or at least can be properly trained.

You should also remove any flowers and flower buds. Disbud double flowering varieties 8 to 10 weeks before the date of the show; singles should be disbudded 6 to 8 weeks in advance.

Many growers switch their biweekly fertilizing schedule to a weekly feeding about 6 weeks before a show. They use a mild fertilizer, such as fish emulsion, for the first 3 weeks, then change to a complete fertilizer formulated to encourage bloom for the final 3 weeks.

Grooming is the easiest phase of preparing a plant for showing, but in the excitement (and often haste) that precedes show entry it is the phase easiest to neglect. Assuming that your African violet show entry is a well-balanced plant, that it has a good amount of bloom for the variety, and that the container is neither too small nor too large for the plant's size, then you should check these details:

- Is the pot clean?
- Are the leaves free of dust?
- Are there any visible insects?
- Are all dead or dying leaves and flowers removed?
- Have you removed any leaves or flowers that show disease or insect damage?
- Have you removed all training aids (toothpicks, wire)?

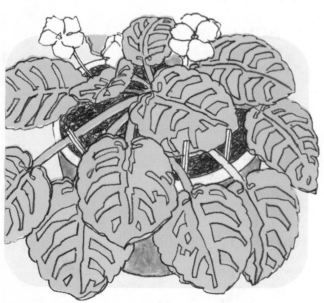

Close gap *between leaves by shifting leaves closer to-gether, using toothpicks as guides.*

Wire loops, *hooked around leaf stalk and inserted into soil, pull leaves down for better shape.*

Thinking Small: Miniature Gesneriads

African violets have no corner on the miniatures market. Many of the other gesneriads described on pages 48–65 also have scaled-down versions which can be enjoyed individually for their diminutive beauty or as components of miniature landscapes.

These miniatures definitely are happier in the humidity and even temperature of a terrarium or other glass garden. Even soil moisture is especially important for the tiny gesneriads that grow from rhizomes; if plants get too dry they go into dormancy and it is difficult to get them growing well again.

The miniatures that are the easiest to find are sinningias. Two species, *S. concinna* and *S. pusilla*, the tiniest gesneriads available, have produced scores of hybrids. Varieties include 'Wood Nymph' (purple flowers, spotted in the throat) and 'Bright Eyes'. When *S. pusilla* is crossed with *S. eumorpha*, results include 'Dollbaby' and 'Cindy'. 'White Sprite' and 'Snowflake' are white-flowered versions of *S. pusilla*. 'Tom Thumb' (white-bordered red blooms) is a true miniature of *S. speciosa* (florist's gloxinia).

If given the right conditions, most miniature sinningias will bloom throughout the year. In fact, *S. pusilla* does so well that it often reseeds itself in a terrarium.

You may find a few miniatures listed under the name *Gloxinera*. This is an old name for plants that were considered generic hybrids—crosses of *Sinningia* (*Gloxinia*) and *Rechsteineria*. Still sold under the old name, Gloxinera, are varieties 'Cupid Doll' with purple flowers; 'Pink Petite' with tiny pale green, hairy leaves and salmon pink trumpet flowers; and 'Ramaveda' with violet-throated pink blooms.

At least one *Episcia*, 'Toy Silver', finds a place in the ranks of the miniatures. This variety is illustrated on page 55. It may take some searching to find.

The genus *Gesneria* includes a few dwarf candidates for your terrarium or light garden. *G. cuneifolia* and its varieties are the easiest to obtain.

Streptocarpus offers its share of lilliputians. *S. kirkii* has rosettes of rounded leaves and lavender to purple trumpetlike blossoms. *S. rimicola* is a curious miniature: myriads of tiny white flowers stand out against a single leaf.

For use in hanging baskets, some specialist nurseries will list two miniature versions of *Nematanthus*: *N.* 'Bambino', with orange and yellow flowers, and *N. wettsteinii*, orange flowers with yellow lips.

Sinningia pusilla

Streptocarpus kirkii

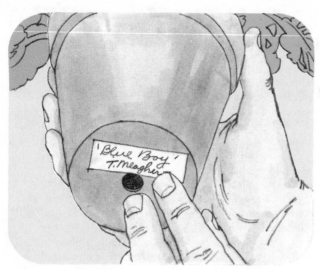

Identify plant (*and its ownership*) *by applying adhesive tape marker to bottom of dry container.*

- Is there a tag on the plant which tells its varietal name?
- Is your name attached to the plant so that no mixup can occur following the show?

An artist's paintbrush can be one of your greatest grooming aids. Use it to whisk away dust, soil particles on leaves, and insects.

To keep your name with your plant, one of the easiest methods involves only an ordinary pencil (whose writing will not smear or vanish if it gets wet) and a piece of adhesive tape. Write your name on the tape and attach the tape to the bottom of the plant's pot.

Getting It There—In One Piece

Your weeks or months of loving care and careful training are only time wasted if you cannot safely transport your African violets to the show site. What could be more heartbreaking than the perfect symmetry of a plant ruined by the breakage of one or more leaves when you had to make a quick stop or sudden turn on your way to the show? What you need, then, is a transporting device in which your plants will stand upright, always remain apart from one another, and will not be damaged even if the carrier should slide around.

While there are probably many ways in which you could get your plants to a show undamaged, there is one time-tested method which bears re-

Pinch or break off suckers *before they grow so large that they interfere with plant's symmetry.*

peating because it is simple and uses materials available to almost everyone. All you need are two cardboard boxes (one several inches smaller than the other in length and width) and some newspaper.

Let's assume you have two show plants that you have to transport by car. First, take the smaller cardboard carton and cut the sides down to slightly less than the height of the pots; then cut two holes in the box bottom that will be the diameter of the pots and far enough apart so that the plant's leaves won't touch when the plants are placed in the holes. When you turn the carton upside-down and slip the pots into the holes, the pot rims should just fit so that the pots are held securely in place.

For transport to a show, put the smaller box (with the holes) upside-down into the large box and stuff the spaces between the two with newspaper. Then, set your African violets into the holes; their leaves should not touch each other (if you cut the holes far enough apart) and they should not touch the sides of the larger box. Now, as long as the box remains on a flat surface (like the floor of your car) throughout its journey to the show, it can slide around without damage to the plants.

To make carrier *cut holes in small box, far enough apart to keep plants from touching.*

Invert *smaller box into larger. Stuff gaps with newspaper; then set plants into cutouts.*

Blossom Pictures Are a Treat

Making flower pictures with dried African violet blooms is a fringe benefit for growers. The necessary materials are readily available and inexpensive; the technique is simple. It takes little preparation time to create a delightful and lasting arrangement.

Cut the African violet flowers at their peak—when they're completely opened but not yet starting to fade. The color of the flower you select may change slightly after drying. Flowers that are deep blue or purple retain their color best. Pink and red flowers fade a little, and white flowers may turn ivory or even slightly brown. Let the flowers dry for an hour or two after cutting.

Spread 1 to 1½ inches of pure white builder's sand (not sea sand), or a special drying agent—such as silica gel—into a shallow cardboard box. Place the flowers on the sand or silica gel so they are face up and are not touching. You may also wish to include some flower buds or stems.

Using a small pitcher or a watering can, carefully pour more sand or silica gel around and over the flowers, covering them to a depth of one inch. Store the box in a cool, dry place. You'll have African violet flowers ready for picture-making in about 2 weeks.

To uncover the buried flowers, gradually tip the box on its side, allowing the sand to flow out very slowly. You may want to dust the dried flowers clean with a small, soft paint brush. Handle the dried material very carefully because the blooms are very fragile.

Before laying out your flower picture, select the frame. Choose one that is suitable for small-flower pictures—an antique, 6-inch, oval frame for example. With the size, shape, and style of the frame in mind, you can better plan your arrangement.

Construct a shadow box of cardboard to match the size and shape of the frame. It should be made ½ to 1 inch deep. Line it with an appropriate background for the effect you have in mind. Silk, velvet, linen, colored construction paper, or even burlap are suitable backgrounds; attach with white milk glue.

You can combine other dried flowers and foliage with African violet flowers in your arrangements. Since African violet foliage does not dry well using this method, you can use small fern fronds or the leaves of scented geraniums. You can also include other dried flowers as long as they are diminutive: small chrysanthemums, delphiniums, violas, and pansies are a few possibilities.

Try out a number of arrangements on a piece of heavy paper similar in size to your shadow box. Handle the fragile flowers with great care. When a particular design pleases you, transfer the flowers and other dried materials to the shadow box. Permanently set flowers with a tiny drop of white milk glue. Gently hold them in place until the glue is firmly set (it should take only a few seconds).

When the arrangement is complete, set the frame and its glass cover in place over the shadow box. Attach with glue or staples.

Unusual Varieties for the Connoisseur

Throughout the many years that African violets have been hybridized, a fascinating array of leaf form and flower color has resulted. Hybridizers have produced scores of varieties quite different from the typical standard African violet. Miniatures, trailers, and variegated types are familiar examples of these different varieties. But there are other, not-so-familiar varieties that could be described as "unusual". The connoisseur of African violet varieties may wish to do the extra searching it may take to find these unusual forms.

Even with the myriad of flower forms and colors, a few varieties have flowers that are unique. The flowers of Fantasy varieties have a peculiar structure: some cells within each flower have a genetic makeup different from the rest of the cells of the flower. The result is a flower that is rayed, blotched, or streaked with a contrasting color or a deeper shade than that of the major color. 'Shady Lady' (page 73) is a typical Fantasy type.

Wasp varieties are aptly named. The flower petals are arranged to give the impression of the delicate wings of a wasp. 'Pink Wasp', one example, is pictured at right.

Varieties such as 'Dardevil' (see page 72), 'Circus Boy', and 'Circus Girl' are representative of a small group that has uniquely patterned flowers. The flowers have a white background with dark colors radiating outward along the edges of the petals. These varieties are not capable of duplicating themselves from leaf cuttings. You must use suckers or flower stems with tiny leafy bracts to increase their numbers.

Foliage variations haven't intrigued hybridizers as much as flower variations have, but there are some noteworthy examples. Scalloped foliage has been exaggerated to the point where distinct lobes are present, as in 'Wasp' varieties (right) and 'Bagdad' (pictured on page 77). Spooned foliage, too, can be quite pronounced, as in the case of the "slipper" types. 'Cinderella Slipper' is an example of this type that has the stem edges of the leaves rolled to form a pocket.

Probably the most unusual African violet foliage is that of the hairless African violet. 'Shine Boy' (pictured at right), with its begonialike leaves, is one of the few varieties that has a smooth surface.

If you're interested in the unusual types but have trouble finding the varieties you're looking for, try these growers: Miller's African Violets, 127 Manor Drive, Syracuse, NY 13241; Albert G. Krieger, 1063 Cranbrook, Jackson, MI 49201; and Champion's African Violets, 8848 Van Hoesen Road, Clay, NY 13041.

'Shine Boy'

'Pink Wasp'

Simple composition *and economy of materials that are all in scale with one another produce attractive arrangement. Foliage used with African violets is maidenhair fern.*

Flower Arrangements with African Violets

A happy by-product of growing African violets—and one that is most frequently overlooked—is their provision of flowers for arrangements. Just a small bouquet of African violets alone in a small vase of water can be surprisingly attractive. Don't hesitate to pick the flowers, as picking does no harm to the plant.

When you work with African violets in arrangements that include other materials, keep in mind how small their flowers are. In larger arrangements, especially, they are best used as decorative fill-in material rather than as the star performers. If you use branches, driftwood, or stones in your arrangement, African violet flowers can be tucked in at the base of these materials to suggest a natural planting.

African violets can shine in miniature arrangements as the star performers. However, their dainty blooms also are well suited for use in arrangements combining other miniature flowers (such as grape hyacinth, small chrysanthemums,

or small crocus), grassy foliage, small fern fronds, or tiny seed pods.

Most African violet shows have categories for flower arrangements that feature African violets. Arrangement judging, according to African Violet Society of America rules, also is done by a point system.

Design of the entire flower arrangement may receive a maximum of 35 points; 20 points are possible for best *use of color*; up to 15 points may be given for *distinction and originality* of the arrangement; 10 points may be given for *relation to container*; finally, 10 points are at stake for the *condition* (freshness and lack of damage to flowers and leaves) of the total arrangement.

A schedule may also have two classes for artistic plantings, in which the entire African violet plant including the root ball is used: dish gardens and terrariums. Dish gardens are plantings in any open containers, that is, those without covers. Terrariums are plantings in transparent containers with the tops covered. Both arrangements are planted in soil. They are judged by a scale of points just for these artistic plantings.

The African Violet's Colorful Cousins

While the African violet has been a household favorite for many years, there are other members of the same plant family that are, in their own distinctive ways, just as appealing for indoor and outdoor decoration. These plants are collectively referred to as "gesneriads," a term derived from the family name Gesneriaceae.

Among the gesneriads you are most likely to encounter are columnea, episcia, achimenes, and sinningia. Columneas are trailing plants grown for their brightly colored, cheerful flowers; episcias (sometimes fancifully called "flame violets"), with their tapestrylike leaves, make exotic accents even without blooms. Achimenes—either trailing or upright—are informal plants that are lavish with tubular flowers, usually in the same color range as African violets; the spectacular, often velvety, trumpets of gloxinia (sinningia) flowers have made them favorite florist shop plants because of their size and sparkling clear colors. Other fine candidates where color and beauty are needed indoors are aeschynanthus, nematanthus, kohleria, alsobia, smithiantha, and streptocarpus. There are also a number of seldom-seen gesneriads such as alloplectus and nautilocalyx, gesneria and chirita—species that are outstanding collectors' items and terrarium subjects.

All of the plants mentioned in this chapter are fine companion plants for your African violets. Generally they respond to the same kind of conditions as African violets do, although each has its own idiosyncrasies. Some of the larger of these gesneriads—aeschynanthus, columnea, kohleria—possess a virtue not shared by African violets: They can be easily used outdoors to decorate sheltered patio and porch areas.

The Dormancy Period

A period of dormancy comes naturally to most gesneriads—a fact you'll find reassuring when your gloxinia starts to sag. African violets signal their need for rest simply by refusing to flower for a short period. But other gesneriads may surprise you with their distressed appearances during dormancy.

The gesneriads with fibrous roots (the same type as African violet roots) have varied ways of letting you know that it's time for their dormant period. Episcia loses its lower leaves and stops new growth altogether. Alloplectus may drop all its leaves. Columnea and streptocarpus will probably take on a shabby appearance.

The resting period for these kinds usually follows the heavy flowering season. When all the flowers are gone, water less frequently and withhold all fertilizer. Resume normal watering and feeding when the plants begin to show signs of new growth.

Expect a more pronounced dormancy in gesneriads with tubers or rhizomes, such as achimenes, kohleria, and sinningia. All foliage will gradually die away (as this happens, gradually decrease the amount of water and fertilizer). When the plant has totally collapsed and all the foliage is dead, store the tubers or rhizomes in a cool dry place (a temperature range of 50° to 60° is preferred). Keep the tubers or rhizomes in their pots, if you like, or remove them and store them in vermiculite or peat moss. An occasional misting will help prevent shriveling of the resting tubers or rhizomes. When new sprouts appear, repot in new soil and place the pot in a suitable growing area.

Achimenes

Throughout the summer, the species and hybrids of achimenes will give you a continuous supply of cheerful, colorful flowers—a feat that seems nearly impossible when you think of the tiny rhizomes you planted only a few months earlier. Their flowers are tubular but flare out to a 5-lobed flattish face 1 to 3 inches across, making them look somewhat like small petunias; there are also varieties with double flowers. Colors include all the African violet shades with the addition of bright red, orange, and yellow. The plants are slender stemmed with roundish or oval leaves of bright to dark green.

During the more than 100 years they have been in cultivation, many hybrids have been produced. These (and the parent species) fall into three general growth categories: upright (sometimes nearly to 3 feet); trailing; and fairly compact, bushy types that are intermediate between the previous two. The smaller and trailing kinds are lovely when grown to trail over the edges of a hanging basket or pot; taller sorts can be used for handsome background plantings in planters.

Plant them in a sterilized soil mixture that is sure to be well drained, such as a mixture of equal parts peat moss, perlite, and leaf mold. These plants must have constant moisture during their grow-ing season (otherwise they will go dormant), but they will not tolerate a water-logged soil.

In early spring when you receive the rhizomes, plant 5 or 6 of them to a 6-inch pot, each one about ½ to 1 inch beneath the soil surface. To begin growth they need a 60° to 70° temperature; when growth shows, move plants to a partially shaded spot and keep them well watered. Pinching out the growth tips when plants are about 3 inches tall will promote bushier growth.

When plants begin to go dormant in fall, let the soil dry out so the rhizomes will be properly cured for winter. You can leave the rhizomes in the pot (without water) over winter and resume watering in spring; or you may prefer to take them out of their soil, store them in vermiculite in a cool dry place, then repot in spring.

Here are some of the outstanding achimenes species and hybrids that you can buy from specialists. Following the name of each is a letter which will tell you if the plant is compact (C), intermediate height suitable for pots or baskets (I), or tall (T).

Achimenes 'Adelaide' (I). An ideal basket plant with many large, gold-throated lavender flowers.

A. 'Ambroise Verschaffelt' (C). A Swiss hybrid outstanding for the tracery of purple veining on the white flattish face of the flowers.

A. 'Camillo Brozzoni' (C). The many small flowers are pale purple with white throats speckled with yellow and violet.

A. 'Crimson Glory' (T). Large flowers colored crimson with an orange to orange red throat marked with light red.

A. dulcis (T). A profuse bloomer; flowers pure white or white with yellow throat; foliage smooth and shiny.

A. fimbriata (I). Small white deeply fringed blooms.

A. flava (I). Small golden yellow blooms on rangy plants.

A. grandiflora (I). Purple flowers with white throats, sturdy stems; attractive red-veined leaves.

A. 'Lady Lyttelton' (T). Red purple flowers have prominent gold throats.

A. 'Lavender Queen' (T). Large tubular flowers, violet blending into a white throat that is touched with yellow.

A. longiflora (T). Flat brilliant blue flowers; largest flower of achimenes.

A. 'Master Ingram' (T). Distinctive long orange tubes end in yellow-throated crimson flowers.

A. patens 'Major' (I). Flowers are very large, in an intense shade of purple.

A. 'Pulchella' (I). Numerous pale red blossoms.

A. 'Purple King' (I). Large purple flowers have pale lavender throats minutely dotted red; very free flowering.

A. 'Violacea Semiplena' (C). Deep purple, semi-double flowers on a dwarf plant.

A. 'Vivid' (I). A spectacular variety for baskets; orange-tubed magenta flowers.

A. 'Wetterlow's Triumph' (T). Very large flat flowers, salmon pink with red markings in the center of a golden yellow throat.

A. 'Yellow Beauty' (C). Bright butter yellow bloom; dark foliage.

Achimenes hybrids

A. speciosus

A. micranthus

A. marmoratus

A. 'Black Pagoda'

Aeschynanthus

You may find plants of aeschynanthus masquerading under the incorrect name *Trichosporum*. The species are native to Southeast Asia and might be considered the Old World counterpart of the tropical American columneas. Their trailing growth is well suited to hanging baskets, from which you can see easily their brilliant tubular flowers and (in some species) attractively mottled foliage. Aeschynanthus prefers higher temperatures, more humidity, and more light than most other gesneriads; its best development usually is in greenhouses.

Most nurseries regularly handle a few of the following species; many more of these species are available from most specialty growers (see page 66).

Aeschynanthus 'Black Pagoda'. Easily produced clusters of red black and yellow flowers; their dark green leaves are marbled with maroon.

A. pulcher

A. ellipticus. Clusters of flaring flowers, light peach to salmon pink; leaves small, oval, and closely set.

A. lobbianus. Hairy, brilliant red flowers with a yellow throat and maroon purple flower tube; dark green leaves have maroon cast. This species is now classified as *A. radicans*, but plants are still sold as *A. lobbianus*.

A. marmoratus. Medium green leaves, beautifully mottled with deep maroon, particularly on the undersides.

A. micranthus. Many small, very narrow dark red flowers; compact, trailing, very thick foliage.

A. obconicus. Bright red flowers; long-lasting chocolate maroon bell-shaped flower tubes.

A. pulcher. Very much like *A. lobbianus* but flowers are not fuzzy. Blooms easily indoors.

A. radicans. Bright red and yellow flowers; small round leaves. A soft white fuzz covers the flowers and foliage.

A. speciosus. Very showy, brilliant yellow, orange, and red flowers. Large fleshy, pointed leaves.

A. 'Splendidus'. Very large clusters of large flowers, orange with dark maroon markings; spectacular in bloom; large shiny, pointed leaves.

A. tricolor. Clusters of small flowers, striped red, yellow, and purple; small round leaves.

Alsobia

Formerly considered episcias, alsobias include one popular house plant, a colorful vigorous trailer, and a hybrid from the two. These Mexican natives are creeping plants, ideal for hanging baskets or large terrariums. In hanging baskets they'll reach considerable lengths if given the room.

Culture is the same as for episcia (see page 54), but keep in mind that alsobias have a more pronounced trailing habit and so require more room vertically or horizontally.

Alsobia dianthiflora is the popular house plant. "Lace-flower vine" and "cat's whiskers" are apt names for this plant—the glistening white flowers are deeply fringed and profusely produced. It has small, light green, fuzzy leaves.

A. punctata is a larger plant with fringed white blooms spotted with red purple. Its larger leaves are toothed and fuzzy. The stems eventually become woody.

A. 'Cygnet' is the hybrid from the two species. It too has fuzzy leaves but they are halfway between the two species in size. The flowers are faintly spotted with purple.

A. dianthiflora

A. 'Cygnet'

Columnea

All of the more than 150 columnea species are native to the tropics of Central and South America and the West Indies, where often they grow in the company of native orchids. Although some columneas are shrubby and spreading to upright, the majority of species and hybrids have relaxed, trailing stems which suit them well for growing in hanging planters. There is considerable foliage variation among the many species and hybrids—from those with tiny, buttonlike leaves to others that have large pointed leaves, either glossy or hairy—but in all cases their foliage is good looking.

But even though the leaves are attractive, it is the brilliant flowers which make these plants really desirable: bright red, orange, yellow, and combinations of these colors. Individual blooms are tubular and as much as 3 inches long, with long, overhanging upper lobes. Some species and hybrids bloom in spring, others in summer; many of the recent hybrids flower intermittently throughout the year.

C. 'Robin'

Because these are mainly epiphytic plants that often grow on trees in their native lands, a loose, gravelly soil is best for them. Add small pebbles, sand, or perlite to a commercial African violet soil mixture to achieve a suitable loose soil structure.

Columneas will flourish in temperatures slightly cooler than you would give African violets (about 55° to 60°) with a ten-degree variation between day and night readings; otherwise their culture is virtually the same.

You can start new plants from tip cuttings of young growth, using the same rooting media as described on page 32.

Regular nurseries offer a few of the columnea hybrids and species listed here; specialty nurseries offer these and many more.

Columnea arguta. Small, leathery, olive green leaves densely set on long, draping slender stems; large orange red flowers with yellow stripes inside.

C. 'Canary'. Bright canary yellow flowers covered with silky white hairs; smooth dark green leaves that are red beneath. Almost everblooming.

C. 'Cascadilla'. Very large deep red orange flowers; small dark green leaves. Everblooming.

C. 'Cayugan'. Large dark orange flowers with red hairs; narrow, glossy leaves. Blooms profusely winter to spring.

C. 'Chocolate Soldier'. Large red flowers; chocolate red leaves. Everblooming.

C. 'Early Bird'. Orange red flowers with yellow base; small waxy overlapping leaves. Everblooming.

C. erythrophaea. Long-lasting deep rusty orange flowers; small dark green leaves. Everblooming.

C. 'Flamingo'. Slender white and pink flowers; narrow bright green leaves on compact plant. Everblooming.

C. gloriosa. Very large scarlet

C. 'Inca Gold'

blooms with yellow throats; small deep green to purple leaves with red hairs. Almost everblooming.

C. hirta. Tube-shaped blossoms vermillion with yellow throats; small hairy leaves; red hair on stems.

C. 'Inca Gold'. Large golden yellow flowers; dark green leaves. Everblooming.

C. 'Joy'. Cherry red flowers; small pointed overlapping leaves. Everblooming.

C. 'Katsura'. Pinkish red flowers; variegated leaves—lighter or darker markings, cream margins.

C. lepidocaula. Flowers in orange shading to yellow at the throat and covered with pale hairs; fleshy, glossy, deep green leaves.

C. linearis. Rose pink flowers covered with silky white hair; shiny, dark green, narrow leaves. Everblooming.

C. 'Maarsen's Flame'. Small, closely set leaves in light green marked with creamy white and pink on rusty brown stems; large red flowers.

C. microphylla. Orange scarlet flowers, yellow at the throat; velvety red hairs on the stems and small nearly round leaves. Spring bloomer.

C. 'Onondagan'. Large red orange flowers; dark green, reddish-cast leaves. Everblooming.

C. 'Robin'. Large dark red flowers; chocolate red closely set leaves. Everblooming.

C. 'Stavanger'. Flowers red with orange base; small shiny leaves on gracefully hanging stems. Blooms profusely in the spring.

C. 'Yellow Dragon'. Large yellow flowers with touch of red; dark leathery red-backed leaves. Everblooming.

C. 'Onondagan'

C. 'Flamingo'

C. arguta

Episcia

Colorful and often variegated foliage is the primary attraction of these plants, although the flowers are not to be ignored when plants are in bloom. Episcias are sometimes called "peacock plants" because the leaves have a metallic, iridescent sheen; leaves may be silver, bronze, or shades of green, frequently veined or mottled in contrasting colors. The tubular flowers have 5-lobed flat faces somewhat like achimenes; many species and hybrids are red-flowered (hence the other popular name, "flame violet"), but colors also include pink, orange, yellow, cream, lavender, and spotted combinations of two colors. Flowers are borne separately rather than in clusters, intermittently throughout the year with the greatest concentration from spring through fall.

Growth habit of episcias is like that of most strawberries: They produce runners (called *stolons*), at the ends of which small plants form. When growing on the ground these plants will spread over a considerable area. This habit also makes them ideal hanging pot or basket subjects where they can develop into cascades of foliage.

Episcias require culture similar to that for African violets except that they prefer more water and higher humidity. Because of these differences, episcias reach their best development in greenhouses. However, they will grow satisfactorily in the home but will give you fewer flowers. Daytime temperatures around 75° and no lower than 60° at night will keep plants happy.

You'll find many fine espiscia species and named hybrids from which to choose. The following list briefly describes some of those most widely sold or with interesting features.

Episcia 'Acajou'. Silvery leaves edged and spotted with mahogany; vigorous.

E. 'Chocolate Soldier'. Chocolate colored leaves with silvery midrib and veinings; vigorous.

E. 'Cleopatra'. Pale green leaf variegated with brown, cream, and pink, and edged in deep pink.

E. 'Colombia Orange'. Large bright orange flowers; bright green leaves.

E. 'Ember Lace'. Dark chocolate brown leaves boldly marked with pink and light green; pink flowers.

E. 'Filigree'. Coppery leaves strongly embossed with silvery herringbone pattern.

E. fimbriata. Velvety bright green leaves with silver midrib; fringed white flowers.

E. 'Fire 'N' Ice'. Silvery green leaves with pale green veins and edging; bright red flowers.

E. 'Colombia Orange'

E. reptans

E. fimbriata

E. 'Ember Lace'

E. 'Fire 'N' Ice'

E. 'Green Haga'. Many large pink flowers; bronzy green foliage.

E. 'Jean Bee'. Wide silvery green midrib and veinings flushed with pink and red on dark brown background.

E. 'Karlyn'. Heavy dark green, almost black leaves, embossed with silvery green veinings.

E. lilacina. Velvety dark bronzy leaves with silver green midrib; large lavender blue flowers.

E. lilacina viridis. Velvety emerald green leaves with silver midrib and silver pink edging.

E. 'Pinkiscia'. Large pink flowers; quilted dark coppery leaves with silver spotting. Vigorous.

E. reptans. Velvety copper leaves with silver and green midrib; fringed deep red flowers with pink throat.

E. 'Shimmer'. Fern pattern of wide silver midrib and veining with chocolate brown edge.

E. 'Toy Silver'. Miniature, with compact, lacquered dark green leaves, silvery green markings.

E. 'Tricolor'. Silvery leaves with creamy white markings and coppery green edges. Very free-flowering.

E. 'Tropical Topaz'. Bright yellow flowers above shiny, pebbly green leaves.

E. 'Cleopatra'

E. lilacina viridis

E. 'Shimmer'

E. 'Toy Silver'

E. 'Karlyn'

Kohleria

Fuzzy is the word for kohlerias. The leaves, stems, and even flower tubes are covered with short hairs that give a velvety look to the entire plant. Flowers (tubular but with flat, 5-lobed faces) are usually bright and showy; red and pink shades predominate although there are white-flowered species and some that have purple dots contrasting with the basic flower color. The leaves may be plain green or lightly patterned in the manner of episcias. Most kohlerias can be grown either as hanging basket plants (allowing their stems to drape over the sides of a pot) or staked to grow upright. The species come from Mexico and northern South America.

Basic kohleria care is very similar to that for African violets: They appreciate the same soils, temperature and humidity ranges. If you can grow African violets well, then kohlerias should be easy for you too.

Growth is produced from long, scaly rhizomes—much larger than those of achimenes. Like achimenes, however, kohlerias can go into a period of dormancy for several months, and their rhizomes should be handled in the same manner as achimenes during this time. You can encourage them to grow and bloom throughout the year, though, by continuing to remove old growth and by starting new plants from tip cuttings. The other propagation method is to break dormant rhizomes into 1-inch-long pieces and pot each piece in a separate container.

Here are several kohleria species and hybrids you may find sold by gesneriad specialists.

Kohleria amabilis is relaxed enough to be a really good hanging basket plant. The flower faces are the same bright pink as the tubes but streaked with a darker color. Leaves are soft green patterned with purplish green.

K. 'Connecticut Belle'. This compact hybrid is excellent in hanging baskets. Pink-spotted flowers with rosy red tubes stand above velvety leaves that are red beneath.

K. 'Dragons Blood'. This hybrid has very deep rusty red flowers that are spotted yellow. Dark red edges the fuzzy coppery leaves.

K. eriantha. The distinctive feature of this species is the red leaf margin. Flowers are orange red marked yellow on the three lower lobes.

K. 'Rongo'. Magenta marks the face of the rosy white blooms and colors the tube. The leaves are veined and marked with dark green and are red veined beneath.

K. 'Rongo'

K. 'Dragons Blood'

Nematanthus

In appearance and culture nematanthus is closest to columnea, and like columnea is native to tropical America. Flowers of most species are orange (although they are in red and yellow) and are noticeably pouch shaped. Given the warmth and humidity they really prefer, they tend to be nearly everblooming. Swollen joints that occur on older growth will root easily if they come in contact with soil; new plants also grow from tip cuttings. Most of these varieties are still sold under the old name of *Hypocyrta*.

Nematanthus 'Black Magic'. Dangling pinkish orange flowers; small glossy purple black leaves.

N. 'Castanet'. Abundant pink, yellow, and orange flowers; waxy leaves are boldly marked brick red beneath.

(Continued on next page)

N. strigillosus

N. 'Tropicana'

N. nervosa

Nematanthus *(cont'd.)*

N. 'Green Magic'. Dangling pink and yellow flowers; small, waxy, deep green leaves marked red.

N. gregarius (radicans). Bright orange flowers, yellow orange bracts; small, thick, glossy, dark green leaves on a compact plant.

N. nervosa. Red orange bloom; dark green leaves on flexible stems.

N. perianthomegus. Flowers yellow with chocolate purple stripes, light brown bracts; glossy leaves.

N. 'Rio'. Bright red orange flowers; smooth bright green leaves on a compact, upright plant.

N. strigillosus. Tangerine red bloom; small shiny leaves on trailing stems.

N. 'Tropicana'. Many yellow flowers with maroon stripes, rusty orange bracts; dark glossy leaves.

N. wettsteinii. Many waxy orange flowers with yellow lip; very small glossy, dark green leaves.

N. 'Castanet'

N. perianthomegus

Sinningia

Three distinctly different types of plants are included in sinningia. The first and most notable is the spectacular florists' gloxinia; second come the other species sinningias, which are less flashy but no less worthwhile in a gesneriad collection; and third is a large group of miniature hybrids and species. Basic culture is stated in the next section on gloxinias—any differences for the species will be noted in their descriptions.

Gloxinia

Next to African violets, the gloxinia is the most popular house plant among the gesneriads. In fact, none of the various gesneriads can match gloxinias for size and impact of the individual flowers. These are wide, flaring, bell-shaped tubes—sometimes as much as 4 inches across—in white, lavender, pink, red, purple, dark maroon, and various combinations of these colors with white in the throat, on the edges, or as a background for colored speckles. Most of these flowers face upward so you can look directly into them. Foliage is in proportion to the flowers and matches them in magnificence: rich velvety green and broadly oval.

This type of gloxinia arose by chance during the nineteenth century from seedlings of *Sinningia speciosa* or *S. maxima,* or possibly from both. Before that time, all gloxinias had nodding flowers rather than the upward-facing ones which these seedlings exhibited. Because the first to flower was raised by a Scottish gardener, John Fyfe, the type was known as 'Fyfiana'—a name which is sometimes attached to these varieties.

Gloxinias grow from tubers and they naturally go through a dormant period each year when all growth dies back. When a healthy plant produces no more leaves or flower buds, this is your signal that the dormant stage is approaching. Gradually withhold water until the

(Continued on next page)

S. 'White Sprite'

Gloxinia variety

leaves yellow, then stop watering so they will dry out. From 1½ to 3 months the tubers will lie dormant and will need only enough moisture to keep them plump—usually just enough to prevent the soil from drying out completely. Storage temperature should be around 60°. Often new growth will begin that signals the end of dormancy, but if, after 3 months, none has appeared, assume the tuber is ready to resume growth.

Pot new tubers—or repot old ones—in a soil mixture that is rich and drains well. Add sand to prepared African violet soil (about 3 parts mix to 1 part sand) or prepare one using the materials and proportions shown on page 17. Place the tuber about 1 inch below the surface of the soil and be sure the indented top side of the tuber

faces up. Water moderately until roots are established; thereafter give plants generous waterings but allow the soil *surface* to dry out between waterings. If you see, later in the season, that roots have filled the container, shift the plant into the next larger-size pot.

Originally from the South American tropics, gloxinias prefer a fairly warm nighttime temperature—around 65°—and daytime temperatures in the low 70s. They don't demand excessively high humidity (about 50% is adequate), but if your home atmosphere is on the dry side you should provide for extra humidity in their growing area. One of the simplest methods is to fill a tray with gravel, set the potted plants on the gravel surface, then add water to the gravel. The water will continually evaporate from the

gravel and increase humidity in the immediate area, but soil won't become water logged because the pots do not sit in the water.

Protect gloxinias from hot summer sun, but otherwise see that they receive plenty of light and even some direct sunlight during spring and fall. Well-lighted locations promote compact growth; too little will give you sparse, leggy plants.

The same fertilizing program as suggested on page 14 for African violets will also be appreciated by your gloxinias.

You can grow new gloxinia plants using any one of 4 propagating techniques as well as from seed. Large, old tubers can be cut into two or more pieces as long as each piece contains at least one growth eye. Dust the cut surfaces with a fungicide to prevent rot. Older tubers usually send up more than one stem; if you allow all stems to develop to the point where each has at least two sets of leaves, you can remove all but one and root them under a glass or plastic cover. Leaf cuttings can be done two ways: The directions on page 32 for rooting African violet leaf cuttings also apply to gloxinias. And in addition to this, you can remove a healthy (but not the largest) leaf from your plant, cut its main ribs in several places on the leaf underside, then insert the leaf stem in the rooting medium and lay the leaf on the soil so that the cut veins are in contact with it. Under cover of glass or plastic, new tubers will develop at the leaf stem and wherever cuts in the veins were made. When the leaf dies, pot all new tubers separately in 3-inch pots.

Sinningia Species

These species are not as widely available as their flashier gloxinia relatives, and because of this they are seen much less often. They are, however, just as attractive in a more unassuming manner. Grow

S. miniature hybrids

S. concinna

these plants just as you would gloxinias. Three of these species —*S. aggregata*, *S. canescens*, and *S. cardinalis*—may still be sold under their old name, *Rechsteineria*.

Sinningia aggregata produces 1-inch tubular red flowers above small kitten-soft leaves. The plant may reach to 1 foot or more, and it releases a pleasant herbal scent when even lightly brushed.

S. barbata has small (to 1½ inches long) white flowers in which the narrow tube has expanded into a bladderlike pouch. Leaves are about 6 inches long, deep bluish green and prominently veined; the undersides are red purple. Growth is shrubby to about 12 inches.

S. canescens (formerly named *Rechsteineria leucotricha*) also is known by its common name, Brazilian edelweiss. In this species, silvery leaves are covered with white hairs, which show off the salmon red flowers handsomely.

S. cardinalis. Broad, heart-shaped, fuzzy leaves grow in opposite pairs on the stems to form a compact plant. It has brilliant red, 2-inch-long flowers; bloom is in summer, but you can have plants

flowering at Christmas if you start tubers in the fall.

S. eumorpha flowers differ from those of *Sinningia barbata* in having only a slightly swollen (rather than bladderlike) tube; these, too, are white marked with red in the throats. Although the green, 4-inch leaves appear glossy, they are covered with small white hairs; undersides are lighter green and stems are reddish.

S. hirsuta is a compact plant with its leaves covered with silky white hairs. Many flowers are produced intermittently from spring through fall; the white is heavily speckled with dark purple, particularly in the throat.

S. regina is the closest in appearance of these species to gloxinias, but the silver-veined leaves with their red undersides are a distinguishing feature. Flowers are borne singly on stems that rise about 6 inches above the leaves; the nodding, trumpet-shaped flowers are violet with lighter, speckled throats and are about 2 inches long.

S. tubiflora is the tallest plant of this group, sometimes reaching 4 feet. Leaves are oblong, green and hairy, to about 5 inches. Although

it may be reluctant to flower unless grown in strong light, it will bear fragrant tubular white flowers— each about 4 inches long in groups on only one side of each stem.

Miniature Species and Hybrids

These tiny jewels seldom exceed 2 or 3 inches in height and spread from 1 to 6 inches. All flower very freely, some being everblooming. Although most will do well uncovered, all miniature sinningias appreciate the extra humidity provided by an enclosed or semi-enclosed container such as a terrarium—some require it. Decreasing the water will force the plants into dormancy; otherwise they're evergreen. Along with the two major species, we list a few of the many hybrids.

Sinningia 'Bright Eyes'. To 2 inches across; ½-inch bright blue flowers with white eyes; everblooming. Terrarium culture.

S. 'Cindy'. Bloom with upturned face; top petals lavender, bottom white; deep purple speckling and yellow patch in throat; leaves red beneath. Very free flowering.

S. concinna. Similar to 'Bright Eyes', flower violet purple above, white banded with lavender below; throat white speckled deep purple. Requires terrarium culture.

S. 'Dollbaby'. To 4 inches across; 1½-inch lavender bloom. Compact, easy to grow.

S. 'Freckles'. Two inches across; nodding ½-inch flower tube with ¾-inch face, top lavender, white to light lavender below, throat speckled purple; abundant flowers. Requires terrarium culture.

S. pusilla. The smallest tuberous gesneriad: 1½ inches across with ⅜-inch flowers on 1-inch stems. Lilac flowers, always in bloom. Requires terrarium culture.

S. 'White Sprite'. A white-flowered version of *S. pusilla*.

Gloxinia varieties

Smithiantha

The common name for these plants is "temple bells," and it describes well the character of the flowers. They come in quite a wide range of colors and color combinations, carried face down (like bells) in flower spikes at the ends of stems which may reach 2 feet high. Leaves usually are heart shaped and are so densely hairy that they have the look of velvet.

The species are native to the mountains of Mexico and neighboring Guatemala where they enjoy somewhat cool temperatures and moderate to high humidity. In cultivation, they need the same treatment as achimenes (see page 49). Smithianthas grow from scaly rhizomes as do achimenes, but in this case the rhizomes are large and

S. hybrid

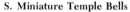
S. Miniature Temple Bells

should be planted one to a container. You can propagate them by breaking up the rhizomes into smaller pieces at planting time or by taking leaf cuttings (as you would for African violets) during the growing season.

Smithiantha cinnabarina is a striking plant with velvety red hairs on green leaves, making leaves appear solid red to red brown. Flowers are brick red.

Cornell Temple Bell hybrids, a series of robust, bushy, showy plants: 'Abbey', salmon pink flowers; 'Capistrano', reddish orange flowers, leaves flushed red and purple; 'Carmel', cherry red bloom, leaves flushed red and purple; 'Cathedral', yellow orange bloom; 'Matins', flowers vermilion spotted red with a band of carmine around face; 'San Gabriel', orange bloom, leaves dark green flushed with red and purple; 'Santa Barbara', buff orange bloom with pale yellow throat, leaves flushed and mottled with red and purple; 'Santa Clara', deep salmon apricot bloom with creamy white throat, deep bronze leaves; 'Vespers', orange red bloom.

Miniature Temple Bell hybrids are much smaller than the Cornell hybrids: 'Little Tudor' has orange red blooms, yellow beneath; the foliage is beautifully marked with green areas covered with silver hairs and plum purple mottling covered with purple hairs. 'Little Wonder' has a rose bloom, yellow beneath, lined with red, and speckled with maroon; the leaves are mottled a deep bronzy green with reddish wine veins that are covered with wine red hairs.

Streptocarpus

"Cape primrose" is the name applied to many of these plants, referring to the primroselike appearance of some species and to the homeland of the first species discovered—South Africa, once generally called the Cape of Good Hope or simply "the Cape." Subsequent discoveries revealed that streptocarpus species vary considerably in size and shape of leaves and flowers and in growth habit, including some species that have but a single leaf per plant.

Flowering season on mature plants of the most familiar hybrids is autumn and winter. But because many will grow to blooming size within 4 to 6 months from the sowing of seed, you can have plants blooming almost throughout the year. Many of the species and their hybrids are perennials which can be increased by dividing the multiple crowns (as you would African violets) after the blooming period to perpetuate favorite ones.

A temperature range slightly cooler than you would give African violets (about 55° to 60°) and plenty of light without direct sunlight will be successful for these plants. Soil mixtures that are suitable for African violets also will be satisfactory for streptocarpus. In addition to raising plants from seed and division, new plants may be started from leaf cuttings. This can be done either by inserting the leaf stem in a rooting medium (see page 32) or by laying the leaf down on the rooting medium so that new plants will form along the principal leaf veins.

Streptocarpus rexii hybrids are the most widely available. These have long, wavy, stemless leaves which in time form clumps of foliage. Flowers are trumpet shaped, to 3 inches long and 2 inches across, in white, pink, purple, red, and blue—often marked with a contrasting color in their throats.

S. Constant Nymph types have delicate-looking flowers that rise high above the compact foliage. Colors are often pastel shades with darker veining on the lower petals and usually yellow in the throat.

S. saxorum has inch-long, very hairy leaves on trailing stems which drape well from hanging baskets. Its white-throated lavender flowers are trumpet shaped and are borne at the ends of pendent flower stalks.

S. rexii hybrids

S. 'Purple Nymph'

S. 'Netta Nymph'

Other Gesneriads

Specialists offer many other gesneriads that make attractive and satisfactory house plants. Many of these are ideal terrarium subjects; others make beautiful hanging basket plants.

Alloplectus

Still sold by its old name of *Hypocyrta*, *Alloplectus nummularius* goes by the common name of "miniature pouch flower." It produces long, hanging stems of delicate, velvety, dull green leaves. Bright red nematanthuslike flowers appear in summer. After flowering, a period of dormancy may follow where the plant drops its leaves but new leaves quickly replace the old, usually in fall. Give alloplectus the same care as you would nematanthus (page 57).

Chirita

Silver veins make *Chirita sinensis* an attractive terrarium plant. Clusters of small lilac blue gloxinialike flowers stand well above the leaves in summer. One variety has silvery veins more pronounced than the species and additional silver markings on the leaves. Chirita does well with African violet culture although the extra humidity provided by a terrarium or greenhouse is more to their liking.

Codonanthe

Similar to aeschynanthus, codonanthe has small, shiny, waxy leaves on trailing stems. *C. crassifolia* and *C. macradenia* both have waxy white flowers speckled red inside. A distinctive feature of codonanthe is the attractive berrylike fruit that follows the flowers—*crassifolia* has red fruit, *macradenia* white. Provide them with the same conditions you would give aeschynanthus (see page 50).

Alloplectus nummularius

Codonanthe macradenia

Gesneria

These are dwarf evergreen plants with brightly colored tubular flowers—ideal for terrariums. *Gesneria cuneifolia* 'Quebradillas' produces many 1-inch, rich yellow orange flowers with deeper markings constantly all year. Gesneria responds to the same care you would give African violets, but make sure they don't go dry .

Koellikeria

"Dwarf bellflower" is the popular name for this little gem. The delicate tiny flowers of *Koellikeria erinoides* are creamy white flushed with deep pink or rosy red on 10- inch stems. It has velvety leaves with dark red green veins and silver spotting above. African violet care suits koellikeria.

Nautilocalyx

This large group of gesneriads is noted for its attractive, often colorful foliage. *N. cataractarum* is a compact trailer with sparkling, dark green, textured leaves and clusters of rose pink flowers all year; unless pinched it becomes leggy. *N. picturatus* is a low-growing, almost stemless plant with beautiful velvety brown leaves boldy veined with chartreuse and gold; fringed white flowers appear throughout the year. Treat nautilocalyx like episcia (page 54).

Nautilocalyx picturatus

Nautilocalyx cataractarum

African Violets Shopping Guide

Many people get their first African violets from florist shops or from the house plant section of a supermarket. When you have a chance like this to personally select plants, take the time to study them carefully before making a purchase. Look for individuals that have fresh, perky leaves in a symmetrical arrangement on a single-crown plant. Avoid plants that have spotted, stained, or otherwise discolored leaves. These may indicate pests at work, but even if not it means your plant will be less than beautiful until healthy new leaves grow out and mature. As a final check, don't forget to pick up the plant and look at the undersides of the leaves to be sure they are free from insects.

If you are just starting out with African violets, here are a few suggestions. Start out with the varieties that have plain green leaves; they are generally easier to grow than some of the fancy frilled-leaf sorts. This implies no sacrifice of flower beauty, though—you'll find the complete range of colors and color combinations, both single and double, in plain-leafed hybrids. If light presents a problem, remember that the varieties with pale green leaves and silvery undersides usually require less light than the dark green-leafed sorts and those with red leaf backs.

Once you have grown a few African violets and discovered the ideal growing environment for them, you probably will want to add some of the newer and fancier varieties to your collection. The easiest way to get these is to select them from catalogs of mail-order African violet specialists. When you buy African violets through catalogs, you have no chance to select personally the individual plants. Fortunately, most suppliers are reputable and will ship only healthy, thriving plants.

If plants you order by mail look somewhat wilted upon arrival, don't become alarmed; this is not uncommon, and plants should completely revive within a few days. Put the new plants in a light but not sunny place and water them only moderately until they show, by their generally healthy appearance, that they have adjusted to the new environment.

If some of the words used in the variety descriptions are unfamiliar to you, check the special section on African violet terminology, page 9. Varieties described as "large" are those that may grow over 16 inches across. The following varieties are grouped according to their flower color (white, pink, and so on) or special growth habit (miniature, trailer).

Where to shop for African Violets

Many nurseries, florist shops, and even department stores and supermarkets carry a few African violets for sale. However, you'll find the largest and most varied selections of African violets at nurseries that specialize in these plants. The following list includes a few of the largest growers who publish catalogs and who can ship plants to you. There will be a small charge for some catalogs.

Buell's Greenhouses, Inc., P. O. Box 218-AV85, Eastford, CT 06242. Gesneriad specialist also.

Fischer African Violets, Oak Avenue, Department AV, Linwood, NJ 08221.

Kartuz Greenhouses, 1408 Sunset Drive, Vista, CA 92083. Gesneriad specialist also.

Lyndon Lyon, 14 Mutchler Street, Dolgeville, NY 13329.

Tinari Greenhouses, Box 190, 2325 Valley Road, Huntingdon Valley, PA 19006.

White

Butterfly White—white, semi-double star; spooned, heart-shaped leaves, dark green, red beneath.

Forever White—white, single, large long-lasting flowers; medium green leaves; prolific bloomer.

Granger's Arctic Mist—white, double; plain, medium-size light green leaves; excellent bloomer.

Kathleen—white, double; spooned foliage.

Miriam Steel—white, often with faint pink streaks, semi-double to double, fringed, large flowers; light green leaves.

Pure Innocence—white with faint green edges, double, fringed and serrated; quilted, wavy, serrated, light green leaves.

Silver Dollar—white, single; quilted foliage.

Star Shine—white, single, star-shaped; pointed, light green leaves.

White Swan—white, single, star-shaped; dark green leaves.

'Forever White'

'Star Shine'

'White Swan'

'Miriam Steel'

'Silver Dollar'

Orchid and Lavender

Cherry Sundae—pink orchid, single, frilled; wavy foliage.

Edith V. Peterson—lavender shades with deeper purple tips, double, star-shaped; plain foliage; large plant.

Floral Fantasy—lavender to orchid blue, double, star-shaped, large flowers; plain foliage with red beneath.

Lavender Fluff—light orchid with deeper violet edge, semi-double to double, star-shaped, ruffled edged; spooned, tapered, medium green leaves, red beneath; large plant.

Mrs. Greg—orchid, double, star-shaped; pointed, plain foliage.

Orchid Melody—orchid with deeper tips, double; dark green leaves, red beneath.

Touch of Grace—orchid, single, frilled; wavy foliage.

Wisteria—light wisteria lavender, double, fringed; glossy, plain, slightly wavy, dark green leaves, red-flushed beneath; large plant.

'Wisteria'

'Edith V. Peterson'

Pink

Ann Slocumb—pink, double, wavy edged; spooned, rippled, very dark green leaves; large plant.

Astro Pink—dark amaranth pink, semi-double; lightly fringed foliage.

Becky—peachy pink, semi-double, ruffle-edged; quilted, wavy, slightly tapered foliage with red beneath.

Fanfare—lavender pink, double; plain foliage; large plant.

Gypsy Pink—sparkling medium pink, semi-double, wavy edged, extra top petals; wavy, light green, longifolia-type foliage; excellent bloomer.

Jean Marie—bright deep pink, double, frilled, upright flowers; lightly quilted, pointed foliage; excellent bloomer.

Margaret Rose—pink, double, star-shaped; deep green leaves.

Mary C—medium pink, semi-double, star-shaped, large flowers; quilted, spooned, dark green leaves.

Miriam Steel, Pink Sport—light pink-flowered version of the white Miriam Steel.

Pink Philly—dark pink, single, large flowers; pointed foliage; excellent bloomer.

Ramblin' Rose—dark rosy pink, double, interesting center tuft; shiny, quilted, heart-shaped leaves, red beneath.

Ruth Carey—peachy pink, semi-double, fringed; quilted, waxy, heart-shaped, forest green leaves; excellent bloomer.

Triple Threat—bright medium pink, double, star-shaped, wavy edged, very large flowers; wavy, pebbly, heart-shaped, medium green leaves; excellent bloomer.

'Fanfare'

'Triple Threat'

'Ann Slocumb'

'Pink Philly'

Red and Coral

Astro Star—fuchsia red, single, star-shaped; quilted, heart-shaped, moss green leaves, red beneath.

Bonus Babe—wine fuchsia, deeper-colored top petals, double, frilled edges; tapered, wavy, dark glossy green leaves, red beneath; heavy bloomer.

Christie Love—coral, double; dark green, nearly black foliage, red beneath.

Coral Caper—red violet, semi-double to double, star-shaped; plain, very dark green leaves, red beneath.

Coral Cascade— intense coral, brighter toward edge, single; dark green foliage; vigorous grower.

Granger's Red Flair—brilliant red, double; plain, spooned foliage; excellent symmetry.

Helene—Rich burgundy red, double; dark green foliage.

Hi-lander—rich coral, single; quilted foliage; large plant.

Inca Maid—red, single; girl foliage.

Mary D—vibrant dark red, double, star-shaped; plain, quilted, pointed foliage; symmetrical grower.

Red Star—red, single, star-shaped; quilted foliage.

Tina—brilliant garnet fuchsia, double; heart-shaped dark green leaves.

'Tina'

'Christie Love'

'Coral Caper'

Blue and Purple

After Dark—deep violet purple, semi-double to double, large flowers; spooned, quilted foliage.

Blue Chips—medium blue, single, large flower; pointed, plain, very dark green leaves; heavy bloomer.

Blue Jean—light to medium blue, nearly single; quilted scalloped foliage.

Blue Power—medium blue with darker shadings, single; pointed foliage; large plant.

Blue Reverie—sky blue with lighter shading, semi-double, frilled; quilted, frilled, medium green foliage.

Blue Warrior—dark blue, single; quilted, dark green leaves with red beneath.

Concord Purple—dark violet, semi-double; lightly quilted, pointed, dark forest green leaves, red beneath.

Exhibition—purple, single, star-shaped, fringed; dark green foliage, red beneath.

Granger's Blue Fashionaire—medium blue, semi-double to double, ruffled, very large flower; pointed foliage.

Lovely Lady—medium purple with deeper shading, single; pointed, dark green foliage.

Lullaby—light blue with deeper shading, double; quilted foliage.

Plum Perfect—red violet, semi-double, star-shaped; quilted foliage.

Richter's Step Up—dark blue, semi-double; spooned foliage.

The King—dark blue violet, double; compact foliage; upright flower stems; tremendous bloomer.

William Bruce—medium blue, semi-double, star-shaped; quilted foliage.

'The King'

'Lullaby'

'Lovely Lady'

'Creekside Moonbeam'

'Vern's Delight'

'Dardevil'

Two-tone and Multicolor

Brigadoon—light rose with intense shading and white edge, semi-double, star-shaped; pointed, quilted foliage.

Candy Lips Improved—white with fuchsia and lavender markings, double; light green, symmetrical foliage.

Coral Pink—deep coral pink with faint white edge, single; plain foliage; excellent bloomer; flower held high above foliage.

Creekside Moonbeam—very light purple with darker markings and white edge, single, star-shaped, full, large flower; light green foliage.

Dardevil—white with reddish purple bands radiating out along the edges of each petal, single; light green foliage; propagated from suckers only.

Delft Imperial—medium blue with white fringe on edges, double; notched, slightly wavy, medium green leaves.

Firebird—deep red center with darker shadings and white edge, single, frilled edge; glossy, wavy, dark mahogany green leaves, red beneath.

Garnet Elf—deep fuchsia with white border, single, frilled; wavy, dark green leaves, red beneath; like Firebird but with better growth habit.

Gotcha—fuchsia with narrow white edge, semi-double to double, star-shaped; quilted, spooned foliage.

Granger's Carefree—light orchid blue with darker and lighter shad-

'Firebird'

ing and white edge, semi-double to double; quilted foliage.

Granger's Purple Crest—white with broad violet edge, double, frilled, very large flowers; quilted, wavy, roundish, light green leaves.

Granger's Serenity—similar to Purple Crest but with smaller flowers edged red violet.

Granger's Swiss Ballet—white with broad blue border, single, cup-shaped, serrated edges; quilted, wavy foliage.

Janny—bright pink with white edge, single, star-shaped; symmetrical foliage.

Jennifer—rosy lavender with darker markings and white to green edge, single, cup-shaped; pointed, lightly serrated, longifolia-type foliage.

Katy Did—orchid violet with darker markings, single; pointed foliage; large plant.

Like Wow—purple violet with darker markings, semi-double, star-shaped; dark green leaves.

Lili Belle—fuchsia red edged with white and green, semi-double, frilled; quilted, slightly wavy foliage.

Monaco—white with wide blue violet border, double, star-shaped; medium green foliage.

Poodle Top—rosy lavender, lower petals lighter, double, ruffled; plain, quilted, pointed foliage.

Shady Lady—light lavender splashed and spotted with deeper color, double; excellent foliage.

(Continued on next page)

'Like Wow'

'Monaco'

'Katy Did'

'Shady Lady'

'Gotcha'

Two-tone and Multicolor 73

'Spinner'

Sparky—deep pink with raspberry red center, double; pointed, dark green leaves.

Spinner—red lavender with white edge, single, extra large flower; dark green leaves.

Vern's Delight—deep violet blue with narrow white edge, semi-double, very large, long-lasting bloom; quilted, pointed foliage; rapid grower.

Whirlaway—violet blue with white edge, double, star-shaped; plain foliage.

White Heritage—white brushed with lavender in center, double, ruffled, fluffy, large flowers; wavy to plain, medium green leaves.

Wild Country—violet blue with trace of white edging, semi-double to double, star-shaped, large flowers; quilted dark green leaves.

Wild Flame—deep fuchsia red with white edge, single, star-shaped, ruffled; pointed, serrated, medium green leaves, red beneath.

'Poodle Top'

'Whirlaway'

'Wild Country'

Trailers

Mohawk Trail—blue with lighter shading, double; scalloped, dark green leaves; semi-miniature.

Mountain Mist—misty pink, single, star-shaped, large flowers; wiry-stemmed foliage; easy bloomer.

Mysterium—purple with lighter shading, semi-double; dark green foliage.

Pixie Blue Trail—light violet blue with darker shading, single, star-shaped; wiry-stemmed foliage; semi-trailing habit; excellent bloomer, good grower; semi-miniature.

Pixie Pink—light to medium pink with darker shading, single, star-shaped; spooned, tiny leaves; semi-trailing habit; excellent bloomer.

Pixie Trail—clear pink with deeper center, single, small flower; semi-miniature foliage; excellent bloomer; miniature.

Seventh Heaven—purple with lighter shading, double; light green foliage.

Star Showers—blue, single; miniature foliage; semi-trailing habit; excellent bloomer.

Sweetheart Trail—bright medium pink with deeper shading, double, star-shaped; spooned, glossy, medium green, wiry-stemmed foliage; good grower, excellent bloomer.

Trail Along—medium pink with deeper shading, double, star-shaped, frilled; light green foliage; miniature.

Tucson Trail—deep pink, double; glossy light green foliage; good grower, excellent bloomer; semi-miniature.

Violet Trail—violet blue, single, star-shaped, large flowers; glossy, dark green leaves; good grower, excellent bloomer.

'Pixie Pink'

'Pixie Trail'

'Trail Along'

'Pixie Blue Trail'

'Dora Baker'

Miniatures and Semi-miniatures

Bagdad—orchid lavender with deep blue shading, double; flat, deeply scalloped, dark green girl foliage; compact miniature.

Calico Kitten—medium blue with burgundy tips, double; quilted, round leaves frosted with pink, rose, and cream; miniature.

Dora Baker—vivid deep pink, double; quilted, spooned, shiny, dark green leaves; semi-miniature.

Last Snow—glistening white, single; pointed leaves; excellent bloomer; semi-miniature.

Little Dogwood—purple with white edge, semi-double; deep green leaves; semi-miniature.

Little Red—deep red, single; quilted, very dark green leaves; miniature.

Little Red Top—fuchsia, double; shiny dark green leaves, red beneath; miniature.

Midget Midnight—dark royal blue, single; variegated, tiny foliage; miniature.

'Midget Midnight'

Midget Valentine—light red, single; lightly variegated, tiny foliage; miniature.

Silver Bells—white, single; glossy, dark, miniature foliage; flowers stand high above leaves; miniature.

Sweet Pixie—delicate pink, double; pointed, medium green leaves; semi-miniature.

Tiny Blue—light to medium orchid blue, double, star-shaped; spooned, glossy, dark green, tiny leaves; plant is excellent bloomer; miniature.

Tiny Ellie—medium pink with deeper shading, double, star-shaped; dark green foliage, red beneath; miniature.

Tiny Fantasy—dark orchid blue with deeper shading, double, star-shaped; spooned foliage; miniature.

Tiny Pink—bright pink with deeper shading, double, star-shaped; pointed, glossy foliage; miniature.

Tiny Pink Bells—pink with lighter shading, single; medium green tiny leaves; miniature.

'Calico Kitten'

'Bagdad'

'Little Red'

'Sweet Honesty'

'Happy Harold'

'Val's Silver Honey'

'Crimson Frost'

Variegated Foliage

Blue Storm—deep violet blue, double, star-shaped; Tommie Lou foliage; excellent bloomer.

Cordelia—pink with darker shading, double, star-shaped; Tommie Lou foliage; excellent bloomer.

Crimson Frost—red with white edge, double, frilled; variegation heavy on young plant, fading later on heart-shaped mature leaves; excellent bloomer.

Happy Harold—burgundy purple with heavy yellow eye, single; frosted Tommie Lou foliage.

Lillian Jarrett—peach pink with lighter shading, double; heart-shaped leaves with pale streaks along midrib and extending outward slightly; good bloomer.

Lyndy Lou—blue violet, single; Tommie Lou foliage.

Nancy Reagan—deep burgundy purple with darker markings, double; frosted Tommie Lou foliage.

Rosie Lou—pink, double, large flower; scalloped Tommie Lou foliage.

'Lyndy Lou'

Sweet Honesty—deep pink, double, frilled, large flowers; Tommie Lou foliage.

Tommie Lou—white lightly tinged with orchid, double; quilted, dark green leaves with cream splashing along edge (can be light to heavy), red beneath; large plant.

Tribute—purple with darker shading, double; spooned foliage with bold irregular splashing of cream and faint pink; excellent bloomer.

Val's Silver Honey—pink, double, frilled, large flower; ruffled medium green foliage with irregular faint chartreuse frosting.

'Lillian Jarrett'

'Tommie Lou'

'Tribute'

'Rosie Lou'

'Nancy Reagan'

Index

African Violet Varieties

Organizations

If you wish to become more familiar with African violets and other gesneriads, you'll be interested in knowing the addresses of three societies devoted to the subject. The African Violet Society of America, Inc.—P. O. Box 1326, Knoxville, TN 37901; its journal is *The African Violet Magazine*, published five times a year. The next two societies together publish the bimonthly magazine *Gesneriad-Saintpaulia News*; membership in either society will bring it to you. American Gesneria Society—Box 549, Knoxville, TN 37901; Saintpaulia International—P. O. Box 10604, Knoxville, TN 37919.

Photographers

All the photographs in this book are by Ells Marugg, with the following exceptions: **William Aplin:** 43 bottom. **Howard Conrad:** 53 bottom right. **Alyson Smith Gonsalves:** 39 all. **Lois B. Hammond:** 46. **Don Normark:** 6, 31 top. **United States Department of Agriculture:** 8. **Darrow M. Watt:** 9.